G000162508

"The Book On Relationship Selling"

Jonathan Bell

First Published in 2011 by
Coniver Publications
Dublin, Ireland

"The Book on Relationship Selling"

Foreword

This is not a textbook on selling "theory." It is a little gem of a book on selling "reality."

Theoretically we try to sell our ideas, products and services to others for our own financial and emotional benefit. In reality, we should be exploring, experiencing and learning how to solve other people's problems with our ideas, products and services, which is always emotionally rewarding and, more often than not, extremely financially rewarding as well.

I agreed enthusiastically to write a brief foreword because I have known the author, Jonathan Bell, up close and personal for many years. He is a valued friend and colleague and is a consummate sales professional and mentor because he learned, early in his career, that the "Old Method of Selling" was doomed to extinction from the very beginning. Jonathan Bell is successful because he knows that you don't sell people what you want them to buy; you serve people by assessing and understanding what they want to fill a need, solve a problem or achieve a goal. To achieve their goal, not your goal!

As a psychologist studying and counselling high performance individuals in every profession - from astronauts to Olympians and world cup champions to top executives in major multinational corporations - "The Book on Relationship Selling" resonates with me because it is the essence of good leadership, good management, good coaching, and good parenting. The principles Jonathan Bell shares in the pages that follow are the fundamentals of all lasting relationships. All relationships are based on mutual respect and unfailing trust. Lose either in the process and the relationship ends.

This book is for everyone because we all are selling every day. If we want to be loved, we first must be lovable. If we want respect from others, we must be respectable. If we want people to listen to us, we must say something of value to enrich their lives. If we want to grow and expand, we must have the goodwill of others passed on to their friends on our behalf.

"The Book On Relationship Selling" does not waste words. It defines relationship selling up front and then gives us the keys to success early in the book:

Beliefs and Goals

Belief is the engine that powers our dreams. Goals provide the compass and targets to turn our dreams into reality. In addition to the principles critical to succeed in the new era of relationship selling, Jonathan also provides the specific action steps necessary to progress from prospecting and making quality appointments, to building rapport through the sale, to turn a customer into a long-term, win-win advocate and fan.

I have followed Jonathan Bell's career for a number of years and can endorse his philosophies and teachings with pride. He has walked his talk with me, my family, business associates, clients and friends by being a living example of the recommendations he offers to you, the reader, in this book.

There is no such thing as a business problem, only relationship problems that impact business decisions. Sharpen your relationship skills and your business and personal life will flourish!

Dr. Denis Waitley, Author
"The Psychology of Winning"

Dedication

I dedicate this book to my mother Lucy Bell, who learnt what it was like to lose financial security when her husband, my father died in 1974. I will always admire the way in which she rebuilt our family life and our financial security. This in turn greatly assisted me in my own life by understanding that we all create our own financial and emotional security.

Acknowledgements

To my coach and mentor, Dr.Denis Waitley, who has been a great inspiration to me over the years. I always appreciate his integrity.

I thank my many clients and their knowledge, from whom I have learnt so much. I now realise that the more I know the more I need to know.

I would also like to give a big thank you to Sean Finn of Sean Finn & Associates. Seán is a written copy expert who gave me great confidence in formatting my thoughts into the written word and assisted me in getting this book ready for publication.

To Zoe, my daughter who has given my life and work so much purpose. Hopefully I can give her that sense of security that my mother created for me.

Particularly I would like to thank Nicky for her love and understanding in my quest to be entrepreneurial in both good and challenging times.

Finally, to you the reader, I hope you will pick up ideas and concepts to help you continuously succeed in this wonderful world of professional relationship selling.

About The Author

Jonathan Bell is a much sought after Sales Trainer and Conference Speaker. He has over 30 years experience in the areas of Sales, Sales Management, Marketing and Training.

Having worked initially in Multi National Organisations, he started his own consultancy in 1994. He has coached and trained over 2500 individuals and organisations to greater levels of achievement and success.

Jonathan is the co-author of the CD series "Stay Motivated for Selling" Seminar and has written many articles on his area of speciality.

He is a long term member of BNI (Business Network International) and is a Fellow of The Institute of Sales & Marketing Management.

Jonathan has been coached and mentored by the world renowned speaker and author Dr Denis Waitley of The Waitley Institute – www.waitley.com

Jonathan lives in Dublin, Ireland.

Introduction

Selling is a communication process built upon rapport and trust. Many of the books that you can purchase on selling show you all the techniques necessary to sell effectively. In the past we learnt that the key to effective selling was an ability to close the sale. Whilst it is important to ask for the business, the real skill in selling is to establish what our customers values are and then to assist them to achieve their goals.

This book is especially designed to help you to build and maintain profitable relationships with both your existing and potential customers. Let me ask you a question. If you walk into a retail store to browse and a shop assistant asks you if they can help, what is most often your reply? Many people will say: "I'm just looking." How do you feel when approached in this manner? Do you feel intimidated? I know that when browsing I do not always need someone to help me make a decision. The clever shop assistant recognises this and will say something like: "If you need my help I will be over at my desk."

The challenge with a lot of the books written on the Old Method of Selling (which we will explore later in the book) is with sales technique. Technique is very important but the real skill is in trust and rapport training.

When introduced to selling many years ago it was the Old Method. Yet I always felt there was more to selling that just closing the sale.

I will take you through a whole process of how you can work with your customers and do business with them more often.

When you consider how often your customers do more business with you, surely the objective of the relationship should be to find new ways to help your customers achieve their goals. You should think in terms of developing a "partners in profit" principle with your customers.

To establish what motivates people to buy is very important and this book will introduce you to different styles of personality. In Dale Carnegie's book, "How to Win Friends and Influence People," he concluded that 15 per cent of our financial success is due to our technical ability and the other 85 per cent is due to our skill in human engineering. In analysing this, it is imperative we recognise that our customers may well not be motivated by the same things or reasons we are.

I firmly believe that the biggest challenge we face as Salespeople is the status quo. Most people are relatively happy with their existing situation or product, and even if they are not, are they sufficiently dissatisfied to make a change? If they are, and we have kept in touch, they may even contact us. What is the price of change? Most people are not normally comfortable with change and it is our business to make it easy for them.

When I started in the field of selling, I was introduced to a method of selling of which I was never a great advocate. We were told to go and make calls and attempt to sell them a product that we had in mind. Now while it got us in front of a potential client, which was the important part, we were never encouraged to find out what our prospect's needs and wants were. Sometimes when we were selling at that time, our prospects bought our product because they perceived a need for it. However because we never spent time identifying their overall financial needs and wants, we often missed many valuable opportunities to do additional or more effective business.

In this book you will learn how to identify these opportunities. When you establish what your customer's goals and aspirations for the present and the future are, you are going a long way to ensuring that your product or service is the solution of choice for achieving their objectives.

When you have finished the book and if you would like more information on my products, services and resources, please visit www.achieve-prosper.com

I would welcome your feedback to what I hope you will find a useful guide to assisting you to even greater sales success. Remember you have the most secure job in the world, mainly because you make it happen.

In the meantime, let's start.

Chapter 1

-The Principles Of Relationship Selling

Topics Covered:

- The Principles Of Relationship Selling
- The "Old Method Of Selling" ("The Hard Sell")
- Win/Win Method Of Selling
- The Sales Cycle
- The Seven Stages In A Customer Relationship

The Principles Of Relationship Selling

Just about everything that you see around you has been sold at some stage – the chair you are sitting on, the car you are in, the ipod you are listening to. At some time somebody completed the sale. The economy is dependant on someone's ability to build a relationship and have people do business with them.

Selling provides men and women with the greatest degree of security to be found anywhere in the world. In a changing era to the industrial ages, where security was provided by working for 40 years for the same company and receiving a pension at the end of your time, selling was considered at that time to be only for those who were thick skinned and for those who had the "gift of the gab" (an Irish expression meaning those who could talk freely). The reason selling provides the greatest degree of security is that you yourself provide it. Your ability to prospect consistently and approach new customers, coupled together with your ability to build and maintain relationships, determines the degree of security you achieve.

The great profession of selling is a highly skilled one. Some people have a perception that it is helping people to buy something that they do not necessarily need or want. In this chapter we will look at the principles of what selling really is and, more importantly, how you can apply these principles and techniques to your prospects and existing customers.

What is selling? This question has been asked many times and here is a definition:

"Selling is an exchange of product, service, or idea to the mutual benefit of the purchaser and the seller." You will note that the purchaser came first and the seller second. The reason for this is simple, if we are to apply the principles of relationship selling, we must always look for a win/win situation. As the great American Sales Trainer Zig Ziglar said: "If we help enough people get what they want, we will, in turn, get what we want." The exchange of a product, service or idea depending on what type of industry you are engaged in, whether it be in manufacturing, financial services or consultancy, it is your job to find out what your customers do and then help them to do it better.

The Old Method Of Selling

When I entered the world of selling, the practice was to tell people what you thought they needed. If you went to a prospect and told them every reason why your product was the best and having done that – you close them down. I am convinced that I spent the first five minutes selling them our product and the next 25 minutes buying it back again. In those days that is the way you were trained. Closing the sale was all important. While I agree we have to ask for the business, our initial job, when we get face-to- face, is building a relationship.

The type of selling referred to above was called "The Old Method of Selling" where the customer was viewed almost as the enemy - something not very useful when you want to build long term relationships with your clients and customers. This method of selling was a by-product of the Second World War.

Imagine for a moment that we have gone back in time to the late 1960s. Let us outline the type of training that took place in those times.

Training was all about closing the sale. Get them to be enthusiastic about your product and then find out every reason why they should buy it.

THE "OLD METHOD OF SELLING"

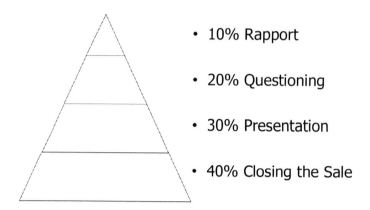

- 10% Rapport

- 20% Questioning

- 30% Presentation

- 40% Closing the Sale

Figure 1.1 The Old Method of Selling

With the model outlined above you were informed that you should spend 10 per cent of your time building rapport. If you could find something that was interesting, such as a photo of the family, you could talk about it. It was stressed that it was important to get down to selling the product as soon as possible.

The next area to cover was to ask some questions. This would take about 20 per cent of your time. The questions you were trained to ask were generally of a leading nature - designed to gain compliance around the product that you were offering.

The next stage was to spend 30 per cent of your time presenting all the features, advantages and benefits of your product. You were taught techniques of getting your prospect to nod with you as they talked themselves into buying the product. This method was sometimes known as the "Carolina Nod" and was used quite extensively in certain industries.

The final 40 per cent of the time was spent closing the sale. You were told how to deal with objections and it was suggested that you do not withdraw until you get at least seven objections. You could be drop kicked through the office window, but you were told to keep pushing for the sale. You were taught techniques to handle objections, the half nelson close, the puppy dog close and many others that always added good content to a training programme, but in fact had no real practical use in the market place.

With the Old Method of Selling, everything was guided towards getting the result. Where was the relationship in all of this? It didn't really matter because the objective was to get the sale at all costs. The name given to this type of selling was "High Pressure Selling" or the "Hard Sell."

Another problem with the Old Method of Selling was retention of business. If these aggressive tactics were imposed, it was very difficult to return and complete future business because the impression from the customer's point of view was that they were sold something as opposed to having had the opportunity to buy your service or product.

Win/Win Selling

The process changed in the 1970s when a new method of selling was introduced because although some of the old methods of selling techniques were still taking place, people started to realise that selling is a communication process that is based upon the trust of the relationship.

How to describe the new method? WIN/WIN should always be our objective. In other words if we help people get what they want, we will in turn get what we want. The motto with the old method was – "get the sale at all costs, it does not matter whether they need it or not, create the need." This brought about the WIN/LOSE principle. O yes we got the business all right and we won but had the client felt that they had lost or perceived that they had been sold something whether they needed it or not? Let us face it. Our perception is our reality.

THE "NEW METHOD OF SELLING"

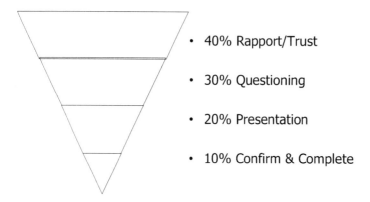

- 40% Rapport/Trust
- 30% Questioning
- 20% Presentation
- 10% Confirm & Complete

Figure 1.2 The New Method of Selling

The new method of selling quite simply identifies that 40 per cent of the time and resources we spend with our prospect or client is based upon building and maintaining rapport and trust. The next 30 per cent of our time should be spent in fact finding and asking questions, which are not of a leading nature.

The next 20 per cent is spent presenting our proposals for completing business and the final 10 per cent is spent confirming and completing the business and discussing strategies for developing the business relationship (process selling). The old method talks about closing the sale, however in reality the sale (relationship) never closes - it is only starting.

When you build proper rapport and trust with your prospects and clients you then have the right to ask questions based upon the trust.

When you ask the right questions, and gather all the information you need based upon trust, you are then in a position to make a presentation or proposal. Finally, when you make a complete presentation or proposal, based upon the right question which is based upon trust, you are in a position to confirm and complete the business.

When you meet some prospects for the first time our job is to defuse resistance, especially if they feel we are going to sell them something. It is a bit like when you go into a high street bank with the bullet proof screens. Our job as Salespeople is to defuse resistance and bring that screen down. If you attempt at any stage any of the old method techniques the screen will go straight back up, into the roof and you may never get it down again.

There are only three ways that you can continually increase your sales and with each of them the development and maintaining of the relationship is of very high importance.

1.   New Business Development

The first way to increase your sales regularly is through new business development. In fact when we start in this great profession, we should spend 80 per cent of our time developing our customer base. We will cover this whole area in more detail in the Chapter on Prospecting. It is the one area that guarantees success in selling.

In conducting sales training seminars for our clients, I always say to Salespeople that they have the most secure job in the world. In a world where job security is a thing of the past, we always have a wonderful chance to make our own security in life. "Our success in selling is directly proportional to our ability to prospect and approach new prospective customers". It cannot be any simpler than that.

2.   Sell More To Existing Customers

The second way you can increase your sales is to sell more to existing customers. If you have been in selling for a while you will have a list of customers who are in a position to buy other products or services from you. While your customer buys one particular product or service from you, they may not realise that you can supply other products to them. It is likely that some customers will brand you as only being able to provide a particular type of product or service. In Chapter 4 we will look at the ways you can introduce new lines of product to your prospects.

3.   Increase The Frequency Of Selling

The third way you can increase your sales is to sell more frequently to your existing customers. For example if you are in the motor industry and the average cycle of a sale is three years, to increase the frequency could be to sell them a new car every two years. What is the sales cycle in your industry or profession? How can you reduce that time frame?

Real success in selling is being able to concentrate on the three areas outlined above.

The Sales Cycle

Let us now look at the sequence of events in a sales cycle so that you can have an appreciation of how this book is assembled. It is important to have an understanding of this cycle, because it puts the sequence in order.

The first area in the sales cycle is prospecting or noticing opportunities. The opportunities for doing business are everywhere, be they direct or indirect.

When we have identified an opportunity, we want to establish whether this potential prospect is in the market for our product or service, so the next stage is to make an appointment. In Chapter 5 we will identify areas to notice these opportunities and how to approach them with a view to arranging that appointment.

When we have arranged the appointment and we have arrived for our meeting the next area is to carry out a detailed fact find with our potential Customer. We will in Chapters 4 & 7 explore how we can identify the GAP of where our customers are now and where they could be by purchasing our product or service.

The next stage in the Sales Cycle is to make a presentation of Solutions to our potential Customer by using a system of Features, Advantages and Benefits (or Outcomes/Results).

When we have presented our Solutions we will explore how to ask for the business, or close the Sale.

The final area in a cycle of constant repetition is in fact is the area of self organisation and time management.

In the Chapter 3 we will explore how you can maximise your selling time in order to reach your full potential. Keeping records of your sales activity can provide you with a huge amount of information when it comes to forecasting your future sales

The success of the sales cycle has, as already discussed, little to do with the sequence of events but more to with our ability to make quality appointments and then build and maintain rapport with these potential customers.

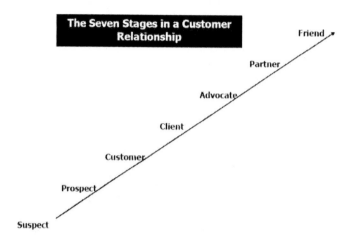

Figure 1.3 – The Seven Stages of a Customer Relationship

The Seven Stages In A Customer Relationship

As we continue to implement the exciting principles of relationship selling, we need to look at the seven very distinct stages in a Customer Relationship.

1.   Suspect

When you identify the name of a person who might have an interest in your product or service, but at present they are unqualified, they fit into this category. Telephone and Business Directories are full of suspects.

2. Prospect

Once they have been qualified under the determinates discussed earlier in this chapter, they become a definite prospect. Once this qualification has taken place, they need to know what product or service you can provide them with.

3. Customer

At this stage a prospect has decided to place his/her trust in the fact that you can help them to solve their problem or achieve their goal. Now how you progress the relationship is crucial. Unfortunately many customer relationships fall down between this stage and the next.

4. Client

To call someone a client is not to be taken lightly. The key to calling someone a client is "rapport and trust". We have heard many times the adage that it is "six times harder to create a new customer, than it is to keep an existing one." I believe a client is someone who has completed business with you more than once.

5. Advocate

An advocate is a client who lets other people know of the great service that you provide. An advocate starts to become a marketing department for you. They will often phone you and tell you that they have made an introduction for you.

6. Partner

In the introduction of the book, I encouraged you to create a "partner in profit" principle with your Client. This stage takes place when you sit down at the beginning of a year and discuss the likely business to be completed in any one financial or calendar year.

7.   Friend

The final stage is where you grow some excellent friends from the relationship – ones that are profitable and ongoing. These friends introduce you to new qualified prospects on a regular basis.

Finally, I would like to finish this chapter by encouraging you to tell all your prospects and customers that you want to do business with them. Tell your prospects and customers that if you are to continue doing business you both need to make sure that it is done properly.

Main Takeaways From Chapter 1:

- Hard sell = NO!
- Win/Win sell = YES!
- Sales relationships are built on rapport and trust
- Sales cycle success is based on making quality appointments
- Turn a sales suspect into a sales friend

Chapter 2

–   **The Inner Game Of Selling.**

Topics Covered:

–   **Believe In Belief**
–   **Beliefs & Where They Come From**
–   **External & Internal Conditioning**
–   **Developing Our Self-Belief**

Believe In Belief

When it comes to selling top performers consistently achieve when they have 100 per cent belief in their own ability. The first sale we will ever make is the one we make to our own ability. The belief we have in our own ability determines the heights to which we soar.

When beliefs are coupled with clearly defined goals watch what happens. Some years ago in Yale University a survey was carried out amongst 100 postgraduate students to identify how many of the students had goals. All the students said they had goals, however when asked how many of them had written their goals down, with a systematic method to achieve those goals it transpired that only four of those students had their goals actually written down with that systematic method to achieve them.

They went back to those 100 postgraduate students some 20 years later and the four who had written goals had a higher financial net worth than the other 96 put together.

With that mix of self-belief and clear goal setting what can you achieve in this great profession of selling?

In this chapter I will give you the ingredients to raise your self-belief consistently and also show you how you can set clearly defined worthwhile and challenging goals.

Beliefs & Where They Come From

So where do our beliefs towards achievement come from?

Why do some people achieve more than others?

Why do some people have more financial success than others?

This concept has piqued my curiosity for many years and has led me to research where our beliefs come from. Some years ago we developed a concept called "The Performance Loop" which identifies why we take action in any situation.

The Performance Loop

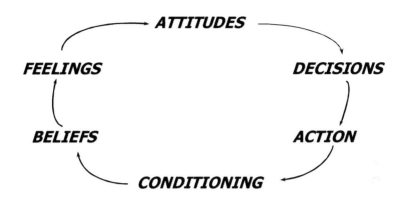

Figure 2.1 – The Performance Loop

When we view this loop, you will see that actions are determined by the split second decision to act. When I say split second I mean that we do not think twice about what we have to do, our sub-conscious reacts so much quicker because it is a repeated behaviour. The decision we take to do the action is determined by our attitude at that time. Our attitude is determined by our feelings and our feelings are determined by our beliefs. Our beliefs are very interesting because they are what we hold to be true about the world we live in.

Our internal beliefs are very interesting because they determine everything we do. If we believe that we are destined for success in selling - that will become our reality. If we believe that we are destined for mediocrity or even failure in selling - that also becomes our reality.

What we hold to be true about the world we live in is determined quite simply by our conditioning, in other words all the experiences that have manifested since the day we were born.

Every experience we have gone through determines our circumstances today when it comes to self esteem and confidence. There are two specific types of conditioning, external and internal.

Typically external conditioning consists of all the outside situations that we have experienced, which ultimately shape our internal conditioning, in other words how those external factors go internal.

One of the greatest examples I can give you is the story of a mother who tells her son Johnny that dogs are dangerous and that he should avoid being near them at all times.

The external conditioning from the mother to the child is that dogs are dangerous and when repeated often enough by his mother this will become his internal belief - habit forming beliefs. This conditioning develops his beliefs so that what Johnny holds to be true about the world he lives in is that every dog he sees is dangerous. Beliefs create feelings or an emotional attachment to the fact that dogs are dangerous, or the fight or flight syndrome which determines his attitudes as to whether he stays in their company or not. When Johnny is anywhere in the vicinity of a dog he makes a decision to stay away from it.

One day Johnny is on his way home from school and he is strolling past a gateway. Out from this gateway runs a little terrier and Johnny catches his eye. With all of the external conditioning already mentioned in the previous paragraph he makes a decision, because of his fear, to strike out at this little dog that is now barking its head off. When you show fear to a dog it is likely to attack and this little terrier bites at Johnny's ankle. The action by the dog strengthens Johnny's belief that dogs are dangerous.

The years go by and Johnny, as you can imagine, has no real love for dogs and at every opportunity will do all in his power to stay clear of them. He is now in his final year in school and is going out with the best looking girl in the class. This is popularity mark one. One day after school his girlfriend says to Johnny that her parents would love for him to come round for tea. He is obviously delighted as approval from her is always helpful. He arrives at the house on the arranged evening and rings the doorbell and his girlfriend answers the door and what do you think is standing beside her – yes a dog (when I use this story on training programmes people always imagine a huge dog). He is asked would he like to pat the dog.

At this point all his conditioning and his subsequent beliefs about the fact that dogs are dangerous come back to haunt him. However, he has to weigh up the odds – if he does not pat the dog what impact will that have on the development of this potential relationship. Also, he may be considered to be a "wimp" – (not a way male teenagers want to be perceived amongst the opposite sex).

Against his better judgement he puts his hand out and pats the dog and the dog licks his hand. At this point what do you think is going through his mind? Well he starts to question, for the very first time, the validity of his belief about the fact that dogs are dangerous.

Using that analogy how can we relate the principles of the performance loop to the world of our sales performance? The reason why some people achieve more than others in whatever field of endeavour is because they believe they can.

When you apply the principles of the performance loop we start to put this whole area in context. Take for example the most important area of the sales cycle – Approaching Prospective Clients.

Have you ever had a list of new prospective clients to call and when you went to pick up the phone you said to yourself: "I'll go and have a cup of coffee and I will start my calls then?" When you return, having had your coffee, does the job at hand become any easier? You see that split second decision to go and have a coffee first has determined whether we take action and when we do not pick up the phone it conditions our beliefs towards the next time we carry out the same procedure.

Why did we take that split second decision to have a coffee instead of starting our phone calls? The chances are that our conditioning told us from previous experience (probably not in the same field of endeavour) that we will be rejected by a prospective client and as humans we like to be accepted, so the easier option would be to have a cup of coffee.

Unfortunately, by not taking the action our belief has been strengthened. The phone has now grown sharp teeth and we do not want to be bitten. You see our conditioning is everything and it is either external or internal.

External Conditioning

Conditioning is quite simply all the experiences we have had in our lives. External conditionings are experiences that are happening around us – our parents, friends, media, television, peer pressure etc. All of these influences can condition us in a certain way. For example a parent might say: "You never finish anything that you start." This is external conditioning.

Internal Conditioning

When we internalise the external conditioning we form our beliefs. In other words we say: "How does this apply to me?" When we are told something often enough we start to believe it. Peter Schmeichel, of Manchester United and Denmark fame was being interviewed once on Grandstand and he remarked that as a young boy he was told many times that he was destined for great things. When told that enough times it had a huge influence on his belief in his own ability.

Developing Our Self-Belief

How do we develop the belief in our ability to sell? In the absence of being constantly recognised by others, although it is nice when it happens, we have to rely on ourselves to develop our positive beliefs on an ongoing basis. Children have on occasion been brought up to understand that "self praise is no praise at all" – only to then realise one day that it might be the only praise they ever get. OK, the reason we are conditioned that way is to prevent us from becoming arrogant. However, be that as it may, we have to work on being responsible for developing our own self belief. We do this in three ways.

1.   Self Talk

The area of self talk is one that is happening all the time. We speak to ourselves 24 hours a day. What things are we saying currently? Are they positive or negative affirmations? When we talk to ourselves we are conditioning our beliefs all the time.

My colleague and mentor Dr Denis Waitley, has a lovely expression when it comes to conditioning: "There are no time outs and no substitutions and the clock is always running."

The first action of self talk is to be conscious of what you are saying to yourself. If you are saying: "I am not good on the phone," be conscious of how that self talk is forming your belief.

Positive affirmations condition our beliefs towards taking positive action. In selling, belief in our ability to prospect and approach is absolutely crucial. We like to be recognised by others that we have this ability. However, reaching the goal of continuous success in prospecting is one of expectation. When you sit down at the phone to make appointments to visit either existing customers or new prospects say this short mantra to yourself: "I am a confident person and I have arranged this appointment with the prospect I am phoning."

Continuously engaging in this type of self talk will raise your level of expectation towards the most crucial activity in Selling − "Making appointments with new and existing customers."

Let us say a prospect calls your office and says to a colleague that they wish to speak with you to purchase your product or service, and you happen to be out of the office at the time and the message is passed onto you, what is your level of expectation when you return the call to your prospect? Surely you will agree that the self talk process is one of complete belief that you are about to do business with this prospect. Consider the fact that if you hold the same belief when you are making outbound calls, it will clearly affect your phraseology and physiology in a positive manner (we will discuss phraseology and physiology in later chapters).

The mind is extremely powerful and will definitely determine your attitude towards approaching new and existing customers. I remember a time when I had three appointments arranged one afternoon and the first two of them went very well. You can imagine my expectations towards the final one. I was on a roll. When my final prospect met with me, my expectation of the prospect doing business with me is huge and this determines my physiology (body language) and my phraseology (my chosen words).

2.   Self Esteem

Being consistently conscious of your positive self talk you will find a strengthening of your self esteem. When you feel confident about your ability to achieve, it will be unconsciously received by others with whom you are communicating. The development of your own self esteem is very powerful. Have you ever noticed someone who when they walk into a room they have a wonderful presence about them. It is not that they are arrogant or that they have a loud vulgar sound, but they have a quiet sense of self confidence.

The next time you are a going to a meeting, take a few seconds before it starts to say a few words to yourself to raise your self esteem - "I feel great, I feel confident" - say that and get into the feeling of positivity, in the zone if you will. They are then imprinted upon your subconscious and let the rest look after itself.

3.   Self Image

In the world of sports psychology one of the most powerful techniques is the art of visualisation. Athletes with their coaches are asked to visualise the perfect event. Dr Maxwell Maltz who wrote the all time classic book "Psycho Cybernetics" called it the theatre of your mind. What does the athlete see - themselves passing the finishing line in first position or standing on the podium collecting their gold medal?

When it comes to the sales process what do you visualise? A powerful technique when coupled with self-talk is being able have the image of yourself in a perfect light , be it completing business with a client, or making an appointment to see a new prospective client.

Take a few minutes every day to visualise yourself in that perfect sales situation. The best way to do this is to find a place where you have peace and quiet. When you have that picture in your mind, hold it there and be conscious of what is going on in the picture.

The consistent imprinting of self-talk, self-esteem and self-image will develop an ever increasing set of positive self-beliefs. When we mix positive beliefs together with clearly defined goals we are really starting to succeed with the inner game of selling.

Main Takeaways From Chapter 2:

– We rely on ourselves to develop our ongoing self-belief
– Positive self-talk helps increase our positive actions
– Positive self-talk leads to increased self-esteem
– Use positive visualisation to increase self-belief

– Chapter 3

-The Power Of Goal Setting

Topics Covered:

- Vision And Action
- Why People Do Not Set Goals
- Setting Clearly Defined Goals
- Being SMART
- Goal Setting Areas
- Time Management

Vision And Action

Over the years, if you realised that once you discovered and utilised the power of the mind in your sales career, then the next factor in sales success is to have definiteness of purpose. This means having a clear written plan for different periods of time into the future.

Let us explore three aspects. If we have great vision of what we want to achieve, but we do not take action we are simply daydreaming. Visions of success may be had in daydreaming but it is frustrating if we do not take action.

The next aspect is action without vision, which is probably what most people engage in. This means that we go forward in our sales careers with no particular purpose. Whilst occasionally squandering time might be good to relax or to let off steam, the reality is that we can and do waste a lot of our lives by having no specific direction in life.

When we put vision and action together we have a magical formula. The vision to know what we want to achieve in different areas of our lives, together with a clear set of actions on how to achieve those goals.

With a clear vision and strong consistent action you will have success and achievement. In the world of sport, coaches assist athletes to have a clear picture of success in an event, developing that clear vision - what success looks like, how it feels and also what language each athlete is using to themselves. The coaches then assist the athletes to define a clearly defined action plan to achieve that goal.

Why People Do Not Set Goals

So why is it that most people do not have clearly defined and written goals with a defined and systematic method to achieve those goals?

1. Some people do not know how to set goals

Goal setting was not something that formed a part of the school curriculum. You had career guidance which is probably is the closest most of us got to setting goals. With a system for setting goals you have a far greater chance of actually achieving them.

2. Some people do not realise the importance of setting goals

Have you ever heard the song with the lyrics "Que sera, sera- whatever will be will be, the future is not ours to see?" When it comes to mapping out the future people do not realise how important it is to have their goals clearly written Can you imagine an athlete approaching a coach and asking him/her to be his coach for the next Olympics, and the coach asks him what he wants to achieve and the athlete replies: "I don't know. Sure we'll see what happens." The coach would be more likely to say that if you do not know where you are going or what you want, then how will you ever get there? If people do not realise the importance of being specific why would they deem it important to have written goals?

3. Some people fear the rejection of others in having clearly written specific goals

The fear of rejection is a huge inhibitor of human achievement. We worry what other people think of us and yet sometimes if you knew how little people are actually thinking of you might become annoyed. When you write your goals down, share them with people who will encourage you to achieve them as opposed to people who may discourage you. When you write your goals down and share, most people will reject them as either a silly idea or will tell you that they are impossible to achieve.

4. The fear of failure

If fear of rejection is an inhibitor to achievement, then fear of failure is really the biggest inhibitor of all. When you write your goals down there is definitely a feeling of commitment. So for some people if they do not write their goals down then they can say that they did not fail. Failure is a fundamental part of success. It is better to have tried and failed, then never to have tried. The head of IBM, Thomas Watson, was asked: "How to become more successful?" to which he replied: "Double your failure rate."

5. The fear of success

This is a real life fear, because we may worry about being perceived differently. When we were in school for example and showed an aptitude towards a certain subject, achieving high marks   rather than things like "well done" or "good for you" we very often heard indifferent terms of endearment - "you swot" and "teacher's pet". Wanting to be accepted by our peers, we sabotaged our own success to have that acceptance.

How To Set Clearly Defined Goals

What follows is a system with which you can set clearly defined goals for different areas of your career and business.

1.   Decide what you want and why you want it

Have you ever noticed someone who has definiteness of purpose? These people know exactly what they want and, more importantly, why having those goals achieved is important to them. If you are setting business objectives or targets it is important to apply a personal meaning to the achievement of your goal. There has always been discussion on whether business/career or personal goal setting comes first. Have you ever heard the expression –

"those people who do not have goals spend their lives working for people who do"? For me business goals are the "what" goals and personal goals are the "why" goals. By knowing what you want to achieve, you put in place a very powerful mechanism.

I sometimes encounter clients who are not clear about what it is that they want. If you are facing that challenge, get a sheet of paper and create a "perhaps list". Take some time out and list all the possibilities that present themselves to you. When you have completed the list, take each of the possibilities and put beside them the personal meaning they will bring on their achievement.

When you have completed that task, state the "perhaps list" in order of priority. By doing so you will find that some of your "perhaps list" brings more personal meaning than others. The exercise will at the very least give you a greater sense of clarity.

2. Set Deadlines

"Goals are a dream with a deadline." By setting deadlines to your goals you start a real process of commitment. Many of us have all sorts of dreams running around our heads. When we attach a date to the goal the time frame really fits into place. Also, the question of achievability becomes real. If you are working towards an event you very often find the deadline is already identified. For example, your sales target for the year is very often the calendar year.

3. Decide the price you will pay for success

When you spend time in achieving a challenging goal there is a price to be paid. It may mean less time on a current pursuit. For example if you want to spend more time increasing your income, it may, in fact, mean that you may have less time to spend with your family. However the reason you are achieving the goal is to give you more time to spend with them at a later stage. Only you can decide the price you are willing to pay. A simple way of analysing the price to be paid for success is to ask yourself the following questions.

- What will I gain by achieving the goal?
- What will I lose by achieving the goal?
- What will I gain during the achievement of the goal?
- What will I lose during the achievement of the goal?

Analysing the answers to these questions will help clarify the strength of the desire to achieve your goal.

Being SMART

To evaluate where you are in the achievement of your goals gives you the opportunity, at all times, to know what needs to be done. There is a well tested method for setting and evaluating your goals.

When you break your goals down into manageable tasks or sub-goals with task deadlines you have the chance to be always in control. When an athlete sets goals they always set mini goals to give them the ongoing feeling of success towards the event.

The SMART method is a very effective way of tracking your ongoing success.

S-   Specific
M-   Measurable
A -   As if now
R -   Realistic
T-   Time Bound

Specific

Specific means having a very clear and precise idea of what it is you wish to achieve. For example: "I have achieved 120 per cent of last year's sales target, so that I have increased my income by 10 per cent."

Always start by having a clear idea in your mind. For example you might identify a goal to move house and you should identify where the house is. So you should write: "I have purchased a house at (insert specific location)......"

Measurable

It is crucial to measure your goals because only then can you evaluate the objective properly as well as having a clear "target" to aim for. For example "I have purchased a new car," is a little meaningless until you identify what type and how much you will pay for it.

As if now

When you write your goals down as if they had already been achieved, your mind is recognising the fact that you can achieve these goals. By stating "I *have* achieved 120 per cent of target in the year 2010," is giving your subconscious mind the information that you are achieving the goal.

Realistic

Who determines the bounds of realism? Only you can identify the achievability of your goals. To assist in establishing the bounds of realism for you it is important to know the difference between limits and limitations. We all have physical limits which we know would be dangerous to attempt and it is important for you to realise this. However, limitations are very often barriers to achievement that we place upon ourselves. The limitations we place can often be created by negative self image and negative self talk.

For example, if you feel you are a good presenter you will have a positive self image and the words that you use to yourself will be of a positive nature. If you have a self-limiting belief about being a good presenter, the picture and the words will be negative.

So what is realistic? What is going to challenge you, if only slightly, to move to the next level of specific achievement? When you set your goals they must be challenging to yourself, to create sufficient desire for you to move towards that goal. If you feel your goal is unrealistic take smaller steps and set an interim goal.

Time Bound

When will your goal be achieved? Clearly identifying the date puts the goal in perspective.

Some years ago when working as a Broker Consultant with a Financial Services Company, attending a Sales Course helped me identify that what I now do for a living was exactly what I wanted. During the course, the facilitator gave us the option to spend the afternoon of the programme writing out goals for what we wanted to achieve in the short, medium and long term. He suggested we go to a place where we would not be disturbed and spend a few hours outlining goals for different areas of our lives.

Now I do not know what my colleagues on the programme did for the afternoon, but I went home and proceeded to get very enthusiastic about my goals. To this day, having kept every written goal in a folder it is a regular event for me to go back and look what I have achieved over the years.

Goal Setting Areas

To identify the different areas in your life gives you a great balance between personal and professional goals. Here are some suggested areas.

- Personal
- Family
- Business/Career
- Financial
- Educational
- Health/Fitness
- Contribution
- Well being
- Travel

- Friends

Before you move onto the next chapter in this book, set aside a half day in your diary to clearly identify and state your goals. Make sure that there will be no interruptions and that you can achieve complete tranquillity. For this exercise to work you need to let your creativity flow and to be at work. This means being in a relaxed state. When you are relaxed and have no interruptions your creativity is at its best. In writing this I have classical music playing in the background. This is very helpful to me in being more creative.

When completing your "perhaps list" set your mind free to flow and write down all the ideas that come to the fore. At this stage do not let analysis creep into the process.

It is really fascinating to see people who have real definiteness of purpose. Those that do have clearly defined and written goals. In order for you to really make, and continue to make, the future happen for you, take this very valuable time out to be very clear about what you want to achieve in all areas of your life. It works – believe me.

Time Management

The old saying from the film "Dead Poets Society" CARPE DIEM has always resonated with me. Looking at Mr Keating encourage his charges to view the pictures of past students who also had the aspirations, ambitions and drive to achieve their challenging goals. To have all the money in the world is nowhere as important as having time. The equal opportunities employer for all of us is time. We all have 168 hours a week, no more, no less.

As a Sales Person how do you spend your time? Here is a survey that was carried amongst a group of Salespeople:

Travel	30%
Waiting	15%
Admin	11%
Sales Meetings	5%
Face-to-Face Selling	39%

In this Chapter we have explored the power of effective goal setting and you broke your goals down into tasks. We will now explore how best to use your time as a successful Sales Person.

You remember my definition: "Your success in selling is directly proportional to your ability to make appointments." Always work towards having a minimum of two good appointments every day. If consulting with a company, it is my goal to have two good appointments on the days when not speaking at a conference, conducting a seminar, or coaching clients. This means that when planning where my new and existing business is going to come from having two good appointments every day helps ensure my business will always succeed.

When you spend dedicated time on the phone every day, you are being consistently pro-active and moving towards achieving your goals. Have a sign up on your office wall that says: "I make two quality appointments every day." (For a free laminated sign for your wall, please email me at:jonathan@achieve-prosper.com

Your Ideal Week

Planning your time helps you become more effective and efficient in the sales process. Planning your ideal sales week lets you to deal with all areas that continuously move you in the direction of your targets and goals.

Before you outline your ideal week list all the areas that are critical to your success as a Sales Person. When you have completed all your tasks, take a sheet of paper and separate it into the days that you currently work as a Sales Person. It should look something like this:

	Monday	Tuesday	Wednesday	Thursday	Friday
7am 8am 9am	Sales Mtng Tel Appts	Office/ Travel	Office/ Travel	Office/ Travel	Office/ Travel
10am 11am 12pm	Follow up Admin	Appt	Appt	Appt	Appt Appt
1pm 2pm 3pm	Lunch Appt	Client Lunch Appt	Client Lunch Appt	Client Lunch Appt	Lunch Admin Follow up calls
4pm 5pm	Appt	Appt	Appt	Appt	Tel Appts

Figure 3.1 – An Ideal Selling Week
Getting the maximum impact from a sales week is very important and something that is worth concentrating on. In order to analyse how you spend your time currently, keep a daily sales log. Even after one week, you will be able to clearly establish if you are obtaining the maximum from your week.

We all have the same time available to us every week. The manner in which we utilise this time is a huge factor to our overall success. And of course that success also depends on knowing where we are going with clearly defined goals.

Main Takeaways From Chapter 3:

- Clear vision & consistent action equals success
- Set clearly defined & specific goals
- Be SMART in your goal setting
- The importance of effective time management

Chapter 4

– Prospecting for New and Existing Business

Topics Covered:

- **The Importance Of Networking**
- **What Qualifies Someone As A Prospect?**
- **Fifteen Ways To Search For New Prospects**

The Importance Of Networking

Having worked with thousands of Sales People over the years, the one question I always ask them is: "How will you get to the market continuously?"

It has always been said that a successful Sales Person is one who can recognise an opportunity in its embryonic stage. In other words you see an opportunity very often long before an average Sales Person has recognised it.

In this chapter, we will explore how you can build a large database of potential and existing clients with whom, over a long period, you can repeatedly complete business. Remember "partners in profit" from the Introduction? Well this is where it all starts. Selling is a process of continuous rejection, interrupted by occasions of success.

Irrespective of the business you are involved in, forgetting that in order to be successful you have to prospect is a route to sales failure.

Depending on your industry, you may or may not have a vast amount of people who require your product or service. Networking with people though is very important because they may well be able to introduce you to prospects that you are not currently talking to.

The motto you should develop is: "Take Massive Action." The world famous motivational speaker and owner of the Mackay Mitchell Envelope Company Harvey McKay (author of "Swim With The Sharks, Without Being Eaten Alive') looks upon every business card he receives as an opportunity to network.

Where are your opportunities to prospect and network? The answer is everywhere. Everywhere you go there is an opportunity to do business.

On receiving a business card I automatically put the name in my data base because if I can build initial rapport with the person, then at some stage in the future they will do business with me. It may be directly with me, or it could be in alliance with someone else.

Develop the belief that it is not a matter of "if" I will do business with someone; it is just a matter of "when."

Building And Maintaining Your Database Of Names

Let us now start working on how you can build and maintain that huge database of names.

What are the criteria that identify a qualified prospect? There are in fact, three.

1. A need for your product or service

Look around you. Who has a need for your product? Is it everyone or is it a restricted list?

The interesting concept about need is that if people bought according solely to their need there would be no need for Salespeople. So is want more important than need? Let us explore.

Imagine for a moment that a man has an insatiable interest in hi-fi. The system in his house has everything - all the latest features. One Saturday afternoon, he happened to be passing the local hi-fi shop and in the window he sees a new system – one with at least one more feature than the one he had at home. He goes "WOW!" Now he could afford to change and he would hate to be left behind when it comes to technology. Does he go for a trade-in using his existing system and buy this new up-to-date technology? Of course he will because of his insatiable interest in hi-fi and his fear of being left behind amongst his hi-fi enthusiasts However add this to the mix. Suppose that he as he left the house, his wife said: "Make sure you get that lawn mower you spoke about so that you can get the long garden grass cut". Imagine for a moment that he does not like cutting grass and does not want to purchase a lawn mower. There is a definite need but the desire to purchase is not there. Will he buy the lawn mower or the hi-fi?

You see at the end of the day people will always buy according to their want as opposed to their need. Remember if everyone bought according to their need there would be no need for Salespeople.

If we consider again that the greatest challenge in selling is the status quo. Why would anybody change what they are currently using? At this stage in the sales process it is difficult for any of us to decide who has and who has not got a need for our product or service.

When we are prospecting it is very easy for us to decide who has a need or not.

2. The Ability To Pay

It is all very well for a prospect to decide whether they have a need or not, however if they do not have the ability to pay the price, the need or want is of no consequence. The ability to identify prospect is of utmost importance

3. Being Approachable

This is not as definable as the first two but is something we do have to consider. It is extremely unlikely you will be able to approach the President of America for an appointment. An extreme example perhaps but, what you have to consider is whether the person you deem to be a contact could become a prospect.

Is Your Prospect The Decision Maker?

How many times have we approached a prospect for a meeting, to find that they are not the ultimate decision maker? When we are at that meeting and we are asking to complete the business and our prospect says to us: "Well I need to get agreement from.........on this". That is a very frustrating moment for Salespeople. We will look at qualifying our prospect later in the book.

Here are thirteen ways to search for new prospects

1. Ask Existing Customers For Referrals

One of the most effective ways to create new customers is to ask your existing ones for recommendations.

Why would your customers recommend you to other people? Quite simply because they trust you to deliver. Developing new customers by pro-actively asking for referrals is, without doubt, the most effective way of prospecting.

Suppose that you are already a long standing customer of mine and I were to ask you for a referral, so as to introduce a Sales Development Programme, why would you give me a list of names? Because you know I will deal with your recommendation in the same way that you like to be dealt with.

To have an opportunity to introduce your product or service to someone else is a great way to commence a business relationship. While this recommendation may not yet be in a position to start doing business with you, this can only be determined when you have made contact with them.

One if the best ways to initiate this process is to identify your top or Category "A" Customers and develop a strategy for asking them for recommendations. In the seven stages in a customer relationship, these are your customers that are in the advocate, partner or friend category.

In asking for referrals some suggested questions are as follows.

"Who do you know that you feel could benefit from the service I provide?"

"If you were starting my job today, who is the first person you would talk to?"

"As you know I want to deal with successful people like yourself, who is the most successful person you know?"

"Who do you know that like you runs their own business in this particular area?"

"Most of my clients introduce me to a minimum of three new contacts a year, if you were in a position to do that, who do you think I should talk to?"

I work on a very simple principle, if every customer, client or good contact, can introduce me to two others I will never be short of prospects, or of people, to whom I will have the opportunity to introduce my product or service to.

2. Trade Directories

There are many trade and telephone directories available to give you an opportunity to qualify prospects. This form of prospecting is the classic way of turning a suspect into a prospect.

This form of prospecting is a wonderful method of initiating relationships with a view to creating long term business contacts. It is a great way of building confidence towards "cold calling". Over the years I have built some great business relationships through this method. Why not build into your plans that you will call five new companies from trade directories every day.

In Chapter 5 we will look at an approach called the "3 Stage Approach" which is specifically designed for cold calling.

3. Newspapers

The next time you open the newspaper; have a look for companies that are advertising. They may very well have a need for your product or service. A coaching colleague of mine uses this method very effectively. He looks at the appointments pages in the daily papers, and seeks out companies looking for Sales Managers, or Sales People and he sends the company some information regarding sales or sales management training. The key to the success of this method is that he is contacting the company when circumstances are changing within it.

4. Join Referral Networks

Referral Networks are a great way of building trust with other like minded individuals. There are many networks that are always looking for new members. Join your local Chamber of Commerce or BNI Chapter (Business Network International). You are actively encouraged at BNI meetings to distribute your business card and network with other members.

5. Past Customers

After good referrals, past customers are great sources of new business. Why you may ask? For a start they know you of old and they know you can deliver and that is why they had dealings with you in the first place. The reason they are not still dealing with you could be for all sorts of reasons. It is well worth your time to take the opportunity to re-visit them and tell them what has changed on your part.

6. Prospects Who Said "No" In The Past

You received an enquiry and you were not successful in winning the business on that occasion. It is very easy for us to say that because we did not get the business first time that is little chance of us getting it next time round. If you can establish why you did not get the business you can adapt the approach to suit the next time they are in the market to do business.

7. Trade Shows And Exhibitions

Whether your company has a stand at a trade show exhibition or not, this is a fantastic opportunity to start building relationships with new customers. People who attend such events are at least open consider what exhibitors have to offer. As prospects, they are actually in thinking mode towards buying what you have to offer and that is why they are there in the first place. Collect as many business cards as you can and write to them after the exhibition and thank them for visiting your stand.

8. Write Articles In Your Trade Magazines

The written word is an excellent way of promoting yourself and your product or service. If you are good at putting material together, get in touch with trade magazines and work at getting your article published. Try to get published in as many magazines as possible. The magazine may also ask you to advertise with them which together with an article make your marketing much stronger.

9. Enquiries That Did Not Lead To Sales

If you are listed in any trade directory you tend to receive enquiries regarding your product or service. While these people may be enquiring from a number of companies, it is a great opportunity to begin a rapport building process with them, even if they do not do business with you first time round.

10. Collecting Business Cards

As explained earlier, when you receive a card, make sure you record the details in your contact management system. Every card you receive is an opportunity to stay in touch with this person. You have no idea when they are going to do business with you, but the chances are much stronger when you have a strategy of continuous contact. You can create a newsletter, an e-zine to send out every quarter, or indeed send them a Greeting Card from a

great system called Send Out Cards – to find out more visit
www.sendoutcards.com/59230

11. Other Departments Within A Company

It is important to realise that when you are selling to large
companies there are many different prospects within that company.
The good service you provide is an excellent opportunity to ask for
other referrals within the same organisation. If you can find out
who is ultimately responsible for the purchase of your product or
service, it is a great start for a strategic selling process.

12. Address & Telephone Numbers From Delivery Vans

Collecting this sort of information is an excellent way of developing
prospects. The van is advertising their product or service, so it is a
great way to start promoting yours. This form of prospecting is
often called "Eyes and Ears".

13. Internet

The amount of prospecting opportunities you can gain from the
Internet is huge – limitless even. By working with the search
engines you can identify companies which need your product or
service. You can obtain all sorts of valuable information to qualify a
company as a prospect. If, for example, you have a number of
customers in a certain area, you can with the help of the Internet,
identify other prospects in that particular area. A good tip for you
when you attend a meeting with a new prospect identified through
the Internet is to print off the first three pages of their website.
When you meet with your new prospects, they will see that you
have carried out your research into what they are about. Why not
sit down on a weekly basis for an hour and source new prospects
with this wonderful mechanism for saving you time in identifying
new opportunities.

Every day, there are opportunities to prospect and identify potential
customers for your business. However, the balance of working with
your existing customer and developing new opportunities will

always be such that they work together. Your existing supporting customer is someone else's prospect and, for that reason alone, it is always important to stay in touch. Your new potential prospect is probably someone else's customer at the moment, so let us now start to look at ways to win their trust and build long term profitable relationships with them.

Main Takeaways From Chapter 4:

- The value & importance of networking
- People tend to buy from want before need
- Always be on the lookout for ways of contacting new prospects

Chapter 5

—Making Quality Appointments

Topics Covered:

- **Being Proactive**
- **Purpose Of Approach**
- **Creating Awareness**
- **Building & Maintaining Relationships**
- **The Expectant Attitude**
- **Preparation**
- **Contact Management**
- **Sales Call Plan**
- **The Three I's**
- **The Three Stage Approach**
- **Dealing With Indifference**
- **The Feel, Felt, Found Method**
- **The 99% Approach**

Being Proactive In Approaching Prospects

Companies spend a considerable amount of money on advertising in the hope that potential customers will not only call them but more importantly, purchase their product.

The key to ongoing success in relationship selling is the ability to meet consistently face to face with new prospects and existing customers.

Recently I was with a company and they had been noticing a considerable downturn in their business. My question to them was how were they were to market. The answer? One of the directors said that they had placed a number of advertisements in their trade publication in the hope that they would get some enquiries. Can you imagine sitting by the phone waiting for it to ring? Well you might get the odd enquiry but do not believe that companies can rely on hoping that the phone will ring.

There are basically three types of people in this world: those that make things happen, those who watch things happen, and then there are those who wonder what actually has happened!

Let us make it happen. Start building relationships. The best way is by picking up the phone and telling somebody what you do, and more importantly, how it might be of benefit to them. You may have called at just the right time. Who knows?

A survey was carried out by a major Life Assurance company in the UK where they sent their Salespeople out in central London to approach people with just one question: "Do you want to buy life assurance?" One in every 69 said yes. Now while you would advocate a more structured approach than that, it does show that if you ask enough people to buy someone will eventually and actually say "YES."

This Chapter will detail a process of how to approach new prospects and re-visiting your existing customers.

Purpose Of Approach

What is the purpose of your approach? Is it simply as some delegates at sales courses have said, to sell a product or service? This after all, is the ultimate objective. No - the purpose at this stage is to arrange an appointment. It would be great if we could identify an interested prospect before we approach them; however, in reality this will not happen that easily. In fact, the search for and identification of prospects who later become customers, is the exciting area in selling. As stated before, if people bought according only to their need, there would be no need for us Salespeople.

It is very easy during the initial approach to start talking in detail about our product or service. Avoid this as much as is possible, keep to the objective of arranging an appointment.

Creating An Awareness

As we have said already there are three types of prospect that we meet.

1. Prospects who know they have a need and want to do something about. These prospects will be relatively easy to meet, because all you need to do is to influence them to do business with you.

2. For prospects who know they have a need, but do not want to take action, creating an awareness is not necessary because they know what they should do, but there is something getting in the way.

3. For prospects who do not even realise that they have a need, why would they have any requirement for the product or service you provide if they do not perceive a need. For this category of prospect, awareness creation is paramount. Later in the Chapter we will explore how you can catch their

attention with a view to introducing your company, product, or service to them

There are four stages from the time we introduce ourselves to a new prospect to when we complete business for the first time. They are as follows:

1. Attention
2. Interest
3. Desire
4. Action

When we call a new prospect for the first time, creating awareness with them is simply to establish an interest. We seek their attention and then build their interest. In later Chapters we will explore the desire to take action but first let us look more closely at the first two stages by building and maintaining a relationship.

Building And Maintaining A Relationship

Under the concept of "it is not a matter of IF we do business, it is a matter of WHEN", it is imperative that we never do anything to tarnish an existing relationship, or a potential new one. Under the old method of selling, you were always told keep handling the objections and they will eventually arrange an appointment. If we create tension within a relationship what happens? Well, we might just be told to move on in no uncertain terms.

When you are arranging appointments always be conscious that people will eventually do business with you if you look at ways to build rapport and trust with them. When working in the financial services industry I waited seven years for a client to do business with me. Now some people may call that undue patience, but for me it was best to stay in touch periodically and it was worth the wait, as they proved to be very good clients.

Remember: "A prospect is a client who has not bought from you yet."

One of the most important lessons to learn about continuously prospecting is the fact that it will bring quality business. It is easy for us to assume who is and is not interested in our product, or service. Rather than us being the judge of that, let our prospects tell us where they are in their thinking. Eventually we will be in a position to provide and it will be because of three words "CONTACT, CONTACT, CONTACT".

The Expectant Attitude

As we explored in Chapter 2 the first sale that we always make is to ourselves. With this in mind, consider the following scenarios.

1. An enquiry arrives at your office that a new
   prospect is interested in purchasing your product.
   At the time the enquiry comes in you happen to be
   out of the office and sales support informs you of
   the enquiry. What is your attitude to returning the
   call to the new prospect?

2. Alternatively, your Sales Manager wants you to
   contact some new leads from a trade directory with
   a view to introducing your products. You have
   never spoken to them and you have no idea of their need or
   want. What is your attitude to making these calls?

Consider the difference in attitude between the two scenarios. It is human nature to assume that in the first scenario you would have a very high expectation of making an appointment whereas with the second you might be more likely to approach making the calls in a less positive frame of mind.
What would the situation be if you took the first scenario positivity and applied it to the second? It may be easy for me to say, but if today you picked up the phone to a new prospect, fully in the expectation of sitting face to face with them, would it not be the case that such an attitude would positively affect the phraseology (words that you use) and physiology (your tone and body language)?

To help develop and maintain such an expectation why not get a large sheet of paper putting it on your office wall with theses words on it:

"I expect to arrange an appointment."

(For a free laminated copy e-mail me at jonathan@achieve-prosper.com)

As human beings we all have a need to be accepted. There tends to be a natural feeling of disappointment when rejected. Mind you, as children we never had that feeling of being rejected. Think about the 3-year-old in a supermarket queue with his mother. Chocolates are often strategically placed (from the child's perspective) at or close to the check-out. Johnny says to his mother: "Mummy, can I have a bar of chocolate?" To which his mother replies: "No son, just wait until you get home, you will spoil your dinner." Johnny is not happy with this. He waits for a few moments and asks the same question, only a little bit louder: "Mummy, can I have a bar of chocolate?" At this stage there is a fair queue forming and Johnny's mother says: "Ssssshhhh, I said you are not getting a bar of chocolate, I told you it will spoil your dinner." Johnny waits for ten more seconds and then roars at the top of his voice: "MUMMY, CAN I HAVE A BAR OF CHOCOLATE?" At this stage Johnny's mother will do anything to keep him quiet and buys him the bar of chocolate. If we analyse Johnny's thinking, do you think at any stage that the fear of rejection entered Johnny's head? Not a chance. He had one goal in mind and that was to get his bar of chocolate.

The fear of rejection, and self confidence, is like an unbalanced old style weighing scales. When our fear of rejection is high, our self confidence is low. When we take action and start to make telephone calls however, our fear of rejection will go down after a while. Why? Because by virtue of our prospecting efforts (no less than ten calls) we start to have some success and our self confidence rises. After continuous prospecting there is no such thing as fear of rejection.

We conduct sales courses regularly where part of the programme is to give the delegates a list of new names to call with a view to arranging appointments. Very often before the phone session there will be someone not comfortable using the phone because of his or her fear of rejection. What we always advise is make just one call to start with. The most challenging aspect of prospecting by phone is simply beginning but once the first call is made and it is clear to the delegate that the sky has not caved in as a result, then it gets a little easier to make the second and subsequent call. Eventually the delegate ends up like the Duracell Bunny – they just keep on going.

Prospecting for new business is a process of constant rejection interrupted by occasions of success. Not only is success determined by our ability to make that appointment, but also by our ability to deal with the consistent rejection. It should in fact spur us on

There is an old story of how two separate shoe companies post a salesman each in a country where people are poor and few seem to have or wear shoes. One salesman views this scenario as a form of rejection, contacting his company to say "Coming home. No opportunities exist here." What does the other salesman do? He also contacts his company saying "Send all you can. Plenty of opportunity here."

So with our levels of expectation heightened, let us now look at preparing our phraseology and put together some carefully chosen words.

Preparation

There are two areas that you will need to be prepared for when in arranging appointments. The first of these is your list of people to call. Remember the fact that you will not know who will be in the market for your product and who won't until you have made contact with them. Only after having called at least ten prospects can you judge the number of people that you will successfully make an appointment with -maybe one, two or even three of them.

The second area you need to prepare for is the time of approach. For some people it is better to call them early in the morning and for others later in the day. If you are looking to speak with executives very often calling them before 9.00 am makes sense, especially before (ironically) the phones start occupying their time. However, in these times of mobile phones and other forms of electronic communication, that any time is a good time to call, particularly when they have phones switched on. Even if you do not get to speak with them, then you can always leave a message and call again.

Contact Management

Do you know how many calls it takes before you get a "first appointment?" What is your ratio of calls to sales? What is your ratio of first appointment to sales?

As a Sales Person it is very important to know your ratios. Knowing them can really assist you in planning your sales campaigns. What follows are some concepts on how to keep your records and always be aware of the correlation between how many calls you make and how many sales you win.

Let me introduce the sales funnel. The concept is based around the fact that the more qualified prospects you put into the funnel, the more sales you will win as a result.

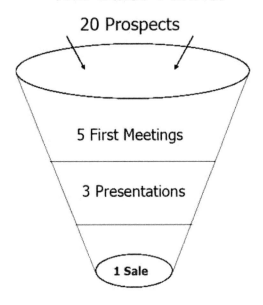

Figure 5.1 The Sales Funnel

If you have 20 qualified prospects, you will from those 20 arrange five first meetings to introduce your product to them. From that you will have an opportunity to present a solution to three of those five and you will successfully do business with one of those five.

Knowing your sales ratios will assist you in planning your targets and establishing the level of activity required to reach them.

Take the following chart and adapt it to your sales call plan.

Tuesday Name	Call	Contact	AS	0.99	1st Mtg	2nd Mtg	Service	Revenue	Referral
1									
2									
3									
4									
5									

Figure 5.2 Sales Call Activity Planner

Adopting this method you will achieve the following:

Calls   – Number of actual dials you made.

Contact   – How many prospects/customers you spoke with to arrange that appointment.

Appointment
Secured   – Here is where you record when your meeting has been secured

First Meeting   – When you are sitting face to face establishing the level of interest in your product or service.

Presentation   – Presenting the solution of how your product will assist them to achieve their objectives.

Service Call	– Re-visiting your existing customer.
Revenue	– The amount of revenue generated by the sale.
99 per cent	–When you have contacted a prospect or customer and they do not feel it appropriate to see you at this present moment, however you have agreed a date to re-contact them.

The benefit of this simple contact management system is you always are in a position to manage and control your activity.

Let us now look at an example.

John works for a printing company and he is on a contract that allows him to earn 30 per cent of the Gross Margin. He has a goal to earn €50,000 for the coming year. He knows that his average Gross Margin on his sales is €1,500 per sale. What level of sales activity will he need to engage in order to meet his target?

First he will need to analyse how many new qualified prospects to be created and then subsequently set about contacting them.

His target income is €50,000 and his gross margin is 30 per cent so his target will be €166,667 for the year or a monthly target of €13,888. John knows that the average sale value is €1,500, so he has to complete 9.25 sales for the month.

He works on the 20,5,3,1 principle so his monthly activity planning will look like this:

Sales	9
Presentations	27
First Meetings	45
Prospects	180

John now knows that he needs to create 180 new qualified leads every month, or 45 per week, nine new leads every day. If we return to Chapter 3 we will see the many ways we develop such new leads.

Under the banner of "TAKE MASSIVE ACTION" consider yourself encouraged you to carry out the activity necessary and let the sales and sales figures look after themselves. Believe me it works.

Phraseology

The language we use is important in getting our message across to people. A study into the total impact of delivering a message concluded that seven per cent is dependent on the words that we use, 38 per cent is dependent on how we say those words (tonal) and the other 55 per cent is determined by non verbal signs (body language). Now whilst this is only a guide, it indicates that 93 per cent of our message is down to how we speak and our physiology.

In my early days in this great profession of selling, I was invariably handed a telephone script and told to learn it off. This in my view was not an approach to be a great advocate of, especially if you did not prepare the scrip yourself but had it handed to you by someone else. More often than not the words handed to me would have been more suited to someone else. It is very important to have carefully chosen words – your own words. Fluency is very important – again something best achieved when you use your own words or style.

You can easily prepare your own phraseology, following certain guidelines.

We are now going to explore preparing approaches by telephone to a new prospect and to an existing customer. For this we will use the Three I's approach.

I – Introduction – (Self, Company, Branch/Area)

I – Interest – (General Benefit Statement)

I – Ither/Or – (When as opposed to Whether)
    And yes we are cheating a little bit by using "ither" rather than "either".

The Three I's give you a simple way to design, and use, your telephone approach to its fullest potential. Remember your first objective is to arrange an appointment and introduce your product or service. Let us break the Three I's down and then we will look at preparing our approach.

Introduction

Realise that in approaching a new prospect, it is highly likely to be the first time to have a conversation with this person. It is important that our prospect knows who we are and what company we are calling for as well as geographically where we are from.

An introduction might go something like this:

Sales Person:	"Good morning, may I speak with John Hughes please?"
Prospect:	"This is John speaking."
Sales Person:	"John, this is Peter Smith calling from the Prestigious Office Equipment Company here in Dublin. Is it convenient for you to speak at the moment?

As you can see from this approach Peter has outlined his name, company and the area he is calling from. Now whether the prospect will remembers your name or not is a matter of conjecture but if you do not give it to them in the first place they certainly won't.

Carefully chosen words as suggested earlier in the Chapter are important but so also is the way we actually use them. Remember, this is the first presentation to your new prospect so it is important to make an impact.

Interest

When we consider again the three different types of prospect that we meet, we can easily define those who will show immediate interest, and those who will not. Regardless of where the level of interest lies, we must assume that there will be interest, so our approach has to reflect that.

You have to use action words and then let your prospect decide whether they arrange an appointment or not. Every one of our potential clients is listening to a radio station called the WII-FM, which quite simply means "What's in it for me?" It is difficult to analyse people's needs and wants before we have even met them. However we have to position our words so that people can identify what your product or service would mean for them.

When you consider what different services and products provide to a customer as opposed to what they are, you can really identify what benefit they will provide. For example a building society does not sell mortgages; it sells people the opportunity to live in a comfortable home. People ask me what I do for a living and it is very easy for me to say that I am in the training and coaching business because that is what I do. But what does it do for the clients I work with? Well it provides them with an approach and method to achieve their worthwhile and challenging goals and objectives.

In the exercises in the back of this book you can identify the benefits you provide to your customers and potential clients. Here are a few examples to consider.

Motor Industry

"Talking recently with Andrew Metcalfe he suggested that I give you a call, as you might be interested in having a look at our new turbo diesel BMW, which has been saving a lot of money for many of our clients given its efficient fuel economy. Is that something you might like to explore further............?"

Estate Agent

"We have a new development of luxury 5-bedroomed houses and when I was speaking with Andrew Metcalfe, he suggested that you might be interested in receiving some information on this prestigious development. Might that be of interest to you.............?"

Web Development

"You may have noticed there have been exciting developments in the area of video streaming, which allows you to promote your company without having to send out any brochure. The purpose of my call is to establish if this service might be of interest to you if not now, at some stage in the future."

Financial Services

"Speaking recently with Andrew Metcalfe he suggested that I give you a call to introduce a new service we have that allows people to make smart choices about money both now and in the future. What I would welcome is the opportunity to outline this service to you and establish if you would like to explore it further. Do you have your diary in front of you?"

From these differing approaches you can see that we have to keep the relationship, or potential relationship, uppermost in our minds. Other additions in the carefully chosen words category would be:

"I'm sure you will find this service to be of great benefit to your business, however I will let you be the judge of that."

or

"I am confident you will like the concept of our new product, however you decide that for yourself at the end of the meeting."

Ither/Or

As we explained, the objective of our call is to arrange an appointment. So it is important that you ask your prospect for that introductory meeting. The purpose of the Ither/Or approach is for you to identify with your prospect when (Ither/Or) would be a good time to discuss as opposed to whether it would be a good idea. Examples of this are:

"When would be a good time for us to meet, would Monday morning at 10.00 am suit, or would later in the week say Friday afternoon be a better time?"

"Let me outline to you when I have time available, I could meet with you on Tuesday at 3.00 pm or on Wednesday at 11.30 am, which of those is more suitable?" I suggest that you choose times that suit you as it always lets your prospect know that you have many other prospects and customers to work with as well.

To help you formulate an approach to your new prospects and existing customers please now refer to the exercises in the Appendix section of the book.

Three Stage Approach

When you decide to embark upon a direct mail campaign, the three stage approach will prove very useful. Also, if you need, in general, to increase your new prospects, this approach will assist in doing so.

From a trade directory, you identify a list of potential prospect companies to call. The first stage is to help you identify a decision maker with a view to forwarding some information. More importantly, it allows you to start building a relationship with a personal assistant or receptionist.

Here is some phraseology for the first stage:

Sales Person: "Good morning, my name is Avril Smith from the Advanced Sales Training Company and I wonder could you help me please. I am looking for the name of the person within your company who makes decisions about the ongoing development of your sales people."

Receptionist: "Oh that is Richard McCarthy."

Sales Person: "Thank you for that. I'll tell you, I would like to forward him some information that I believe he will find of benefit and I just want to make sure I am addressing it to the right person. Would you be good enough to let Richard know that I will be forwarding the information today?"

Receptionist: "Certainly I will."

Sales Person: "Thank you for that. Can I ask who I am speaking with please?"

Receptionist: "My name is Olga".

Sales Person: "Olga many thanks for your help."

Now what has happened in this first stage? Primarily we have received the name of the person that makes the decisions.

Secondly, we have a commitment from the receptionist that she will inform the decision maker of the material to be forwarded (whether that happens or not is out of our control). Thirdly, we have the name of the receptionist or personal assistant of whom we will ask for during the third stage. It is very important to start building relationships at all levels or points within the company.

Second Stage

Now that you have the names needed, send a brief letter to the prospect. Brief means it should only be to introduce yourself and your company. This opportunity is not to send all of your brochures, but a chance to send an introductory letter and an attachment that briefly outlines how your product or service can be of benefit to the person you are contacting. For example at our company, we would include an attachment that outlining: "Ten Ways to Achieve the Best Results from Your Sales Team."

In keeping your letter succinct and to the point, you might consider the following example:

Mr Richard McCarthy,
Sales Director
XYZ Widgets Ltd
Main St
Your town

Date

Re: Assisting Your Sales People Achieve their Full
          Potential.

Dear Richard,

Following my conversation with Olga this morning, let me introduce myself and my company to you.

As a business we are dedicated to assisting companies achieve their challenging goals and objectives. To this end we utilise a highly effective process of Executive Sales Coaching.

I would welcome the opportunity to meet and establish if we can be of assistance in helping you achieve those goals.

Attached is an article which I hope you will find interesting. I will call you in the near future to see if a meeting would be convenient.

Yours sincerely,

_____

Avril Smith.
Sales Development Coach

Third Stage

After you send your letter, wait for a few days and then follow up. We now have the name of the receptionist and this is how we should approach our call. Here is Avril.

Avril:	"Good morning is that Olga?"
Receptionist:	"This is Olga speaking."
Avril:	"Olga, this is Avril from the Advanced Training Company. I was speaking with you the other day and I have forwarded that information to Richard McCarthy and I was wondering if he is available to speak with, as I promised to follow up."
Olga:	"Just one moment."

The stage approach is no guarantee that you will be put through to the decision maker, but it does enhance your chances. More importantly, you continue to have the opportunity to build relationships with a receptionist or a personal assistant. Courtesy is key at all stages.

Use this method to identify how many new prospects you will create every week. There are many people who utilise this method of prospecting on a regular basis. Remember it is the quantity of approaches that will create quality business opportunities.

Dealing With Indifference

It would be absolutely fantastic if everyone we called agreed to meet us and give us the opportunity to introduce our product. Unfortunately it does not always work that way. Initially we will only make a certain amount of appointments without meeting prospect or customer indifference.

Dealing successfully with customer indifference is a master skill. Under the old method of selling people were taught that they do not leave a house or office until they get at least seven objections. In reality think of what that was doing for a potential business relationship. My advice is to take one opportunity to deal with customer indifference and if that is not successful then gracefully withdraw until another time (as there is no desire to purchase at that point).

Here are some of the main reasons why a prospect does not always agree to a meeting during an initial approach:

* Buying the wrong product
* Buying at an exorbitant price
* Buying from the wrong supplier
* Buying too much
* Buying at the wrong time
* Being given one-sided information
* Falling victim to empty promises
* Being overloaded by work due to the purchase

* Being criticised as a result of the purchase.

If these fears are real, and assume they are, you must find ways to help your prospect feel more comfortable and at ease. Realise that your job is to continue to build rapport and trust at this stage.

The types of indifference statements you are likely to receive are as follows:

- I'm not interested
- I'm too busy
- I will call you back, if I am interested
- You are too expensive
- Send me details
- We are happy with our existing supplier

Earlier in the book we discussed that the biggest challenge we face in selling is the "status quo." Our ability to deal with indifference, and keep the potential relationship uppermost in our minds, is paramount. Here is a suggested method for dealing with indifference.

The Feel, Felt, Found Method

It is imperative to build empathy at this stage and this approach does just that. Here is an example:

"I can appreciate how you feel and many of our clients felt the same way initially, however when we met and discussed the real value of this product they were very happy to proceed to the next stage. As I said this new product is very innovative, so with that in mind when would be a good time for us to have an initial meeting. Would Monday afternoon be a good time, or would later in the week in fact be a better time?"

Through using this approach you have created empathy by agreeing with them and at the same time letting them know that they are not alone in their feelings. However if they are prepared to explore the product a little further many clients have found the product to be of great value.

Sometimes feel, felt and found can sound a little clichéd. To minimise this risk, simply alter some of the statements to suit.

"I appreciate how you feel."
"I understand your view."

"Others felt the same way."
"Some of our existing clients were of the same opinion initially."
"However they found the product to be of great benefit."

"The product proved to be of great benefit".

We can argue about the words to be used in dealing with customer indifference. Sentiment is the most important.

Of the above objections there are two where a slightly different approach might be beneficial:

"I'm too busy."

When a prospect tells you that they are too busy, you have to establish that this is the case or whether it is a nice way of saying: "I'm not interested."

Your response could be as follows:

"I can appreciate that you are very busy at present, and I would welcome the opportunity to meet with you. Tell me when you feel I should call you at a later stage to arrange an appointment."

If at that stage they say that they are not interested, you know you are dealing with an objection of a different nature. If, however, they say to give them a call in a month, it demonstrates that there may be a certain degree of interest.

"I will give you a call back if I am interested."

When you are making appointments, it is very important that you stay in control of your prospecting activities. If a prospect says they will call back, you have ultimately lost control of that call. They may well, of course, call you back, but in reality we know how busy people are.

A way to control the call is as follows:

"I would be delighted for you to call me back. However, as you can appreciate, I am in and out of the office at meetings and I would not like to miss your call. It would be easier for me to call you back at a time that is convenient for you. When would be a good time for me to call you again?"

Hopefully they will ask you to call them again at an agreed time in the future. Controlling your follow-ups means you are always pro-active in your approach to making appointments.

99 Per Cent Approach

If, as already said, you do not get a positive response at this stage it is time to withdraw. When you continue to build rapport and trust by giving your prospect some space, which is all they may be looking for, you will always have a chance of meeting them at some stage. The 99 per cent approach gives you the chance to keep communication channels open.

The approach is as follows:

"I can appreciate that this new service is not of any

benefit to you at present. However I hope it will be at some stage in the future. Tell me from a contact point of view, when should I call again to establish if a meeting would be convenient?"

Most genuine people will give a date at some point in the future – so mark that in your contact management system and call back at the agreed time.

As we approach the skills of the face to face meeting, it is important to note that the number of times you approach a potential customer, will determine your level of success in selling.

Remember the entire process of selling is one of constant rejection, interrupted by occasions of success.

Main Takeaways From Chapter 5:

- Always be proactive
- Having a positive attitude is key
- Expect to make appointments
- Prospecting for new business is a process of frequent rejection interrupted by occasions of success
- Plan your sales calls properly – you will be far more successful when you do
- Words – the ones you use & how you use them will have an enormous bearing on your success
- Dealing with indifference is a master skill
- Know when to withdraw from a prospect so as not to damage future chances.

Chapter 6

— Building and Maintaining Rapport with Customers

Topics Covered:

- **The Perfect Salesperson**
- **Why People Buy**
- **The Structure Of A Sales Meeting**
- **Rapport & Tools To Help Build It**
- **Personality Types**

The Perfect Salesperson

Imagine this if you will. In the context of your product or service you have developed a capacity to read people's minds when it comes to their needs and wants. Every time you arrive at a new prospect's office you know exactly what they want and you build an instantaneous rapport and trust with them, which means you do business with your new prospect every single time.

A wonderful idea surely and the more you work at developing your own rapport and trust building skills, the closer you will move to this ideal.

Well you have made your appointment and you are on your way to meet your prospect for the first time. Equally, you could be going back to meet an existing customer, or a past customer.

During this Chapter we will look at how you can view your prospect or customer's map of the world, and find out what is important to them. We will then give the tools and techniques to assist you in establishing how your product or service can assist them to achieve their goals and objectives

In Chapter 1, we explored the Old Method of Selling where Salespeople very often had a pre-conceived idea of what they were going to sell to their prospects. With the new method of selling you do not and indeed cannot have any pre-conceived ideas as to what your prospect's needs or wants are. While you go to this meeting with a competent degree of product knowledge, you have little idea of their needs and wants. Gone are the days where we sold somebody a product that we thought they needed.

Consider yourself a "Doctor" of Selling." A doctor, as you know, would not prescribe or recommend any solution until he or she carries out a full examination, only then making a diagnosis. The same principle applies with the new method of selling - carrying out a full fact find so that we can make a specific presentation.

Why People Buy

First of all, why do people buy? To understand buyer psychology we need to be aware of the many reasons people make a decision to do business.

Emotional Reasons For Buying:

Fear of being left behind
Envy of other's purchase
Vanity of recognition from others
Love and approval of colleagues, family and friends
Entertainment, enjoyment and relaxation
Sentimental, family tradition or local company
Pride of being associated with a successful product
Pleasure being derived from the appearance of a new product

Logical reasons for buying:

Profit, increased efficiency, less wastage
Health reasons, less hazardous
Security of buying from a well established company, buying a specific brand
Utility of being easier to use, or that it saves time
Caution of providing fewer service calls

As you can see, there are many reasons why your customers do business with you. To find out more why not take your top customers and ask them: "Why do you do business with our company?" or, "What is important to you in doing business with our company?"

The Structure Of A Sales Meeting

It is important to have structure in any kind of meeting – having one makes it easier to monitor and judge your success or otherwise. While structure does not always stay exactly to form, we have to have guidelines so as to control the meeting. If you were going to a residents association meeting you would have an agenda. Here is a suggested structure:

- Rapport
- Opening Statement
- Elicit Values
- Determine goals using the GAP Analysis & utilising the P.R.O.S.P.E.R© Consultative Selling Method
- Judgement
- Present Solutions
- Confirmation/Completion
- Outline ongoing process

Rapport & Tools To Help Build It

As we outlined in the new method of selling, 40 per cent of success is determined by the levels of trust and rapport that we build with our new prospects and existing customers. The very first interaction that occurs when we meet people for the first time is eye contact. Be very conscious of these first few seconds because our prospects are looking to deal with people who are confident in themselves. A simple human relationship tip in maintaining eye contact is to notice the colour of their eyes. To do so you actually have to look at them.

The next action that takes place, particularly in Western Culture, is a handshake. Have you ever had a handshake where the hand just slid out of yours? As this interaction is the first opportunity we have to build rapport it would be fair to say that a limp handshake does not instil the greatest degree of confidence. People have been known to say that they only received the index finger as a handshake.

Alternatively, you could receive the "nutcrusher" handshake. The person who squeezes your hand so hard that you spend the whole meeting in pain. What impression is that giving? Some people say it displays arrogance or aggressiveness, someone who really wants to dominate the meeting.

All you need is a firm handshake that displays we are confident in ourselves. Our prospects and clients want to know that we are competent, trustworthy and knowledgeable. Think about it for a moment. If you were not in the business you are in and you have a need, what type of person would you expect to be dealing with you? It is highly likely that you would want to deal with someone who displays such trustworthy qualities.

There are, of course, people we build instantaneous rapport with and then there are others that we wonder about. As rapport is an extremely important component for building trust with potential clients what follows is a method designed to enable you to build lasting relationships. It comes with due recognition to the work of the Swiss Psychologist Carl G Jung who coined the phrase introvert and extrovert. His book "Psychological Types" laid the foundation for the following.

One of the most important aspects in building rapport is being able to see the world from our client's perspective. What motivates your client to buy? Having an understanding of your prospect's personality style is very helpful in building trust and rapport. We will discuss how you can recognise a prospect's buying style, by "reading" their body language, signals, and the words that they use.

People are often heard to say that that they find it difficult to communicate with certain people. This in my belief is not really the case - it is far more likely to be the mere fact that they are not in rapport with them.

There is a friend of mine who when asked a question to which you might normally expect an elaborate response, merely answers quite succinctly. He is comfortable with long silences after that and only speaks when he feels he needs to. However, he does have a wonderful ability to listen to me or others.

Have you ever been in a business situation like that? Is my friend in essence a really effective communicator by listening more than speaking? We have after all one mouth but two ears.

Let us now explore why people do what they do when communicating with others. As Denis Waitley has said: "The only world we will ever know is the one we see through our eyes."

Selling & Buying Styles

Let us look at two initial types.

The Self-Contained Task Oriented Person

The first signal you are given for this type of person is the mere fact that they show little emotion and often have a serious demeanour. They tend to focus on task orientation and often will act in a business-like fashion. Self-contained people often show little emotion and keep their cards close to their chest. They are often viewed as being hard to get to know as they avoid personal involvement.

The Open Person

You can sometimes read these people like a book. They show plenty of emotion and tend to wear their hearts on their sleeves. They rely on their intuition and will often tell you exactly how they feel in most situations. In a situation where reprimand is needed they will think of the person before the result. For the open person "who is right" is more important than "what is right."

You may already be recognising traits of many of your existing customers and clients.

When you look at the following graph, where would you put yourself on the scale of 1-4.?Are you towards being self-contained, or open, in your approach to other people? The best way for you to analyse yourself where you might sit, is to mark yourself between 1-4.

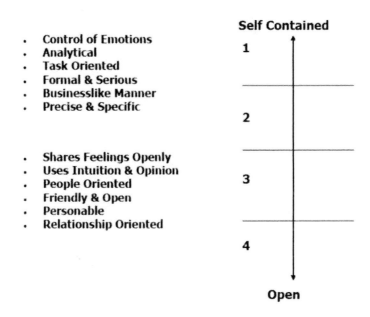

Figure 6.1 Self Contained and Open

We then look at a horizontal scale and on the right side we have someone who is direct and on the left side we have someone who is indirect.

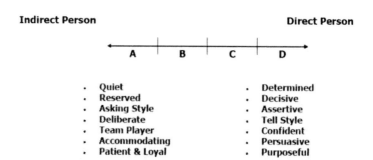

Figure 6.2 Indirect or Direct

The Direct Person

Direct people tend to think outwardly and are very assertive in their dealings. They make decisions quickly and use a tell, rather than an ask, style. They show great confidence and are very impatient to move projects forward. They tend to display tremendous empathy for different situations. The Direct person will rely on gut feeling and will be more likely to rely on their intuition.

The Indirect Person

Indirect people appear to have a greater preference towards introversion. The perception would be that they are quieter and more reserved. They tend to make decisions when they have analysed a situation with all the facts and information, as opposed to making decisions based on "gut feel." They are very good listeners and tend to ask a lot of questions. The great team players tend to be more indirect and will show great support for their colleagues.

When you look at the horizontal scale, rate yourself A,B,C or D. Now we have a vertical scale and a horizontal scale.

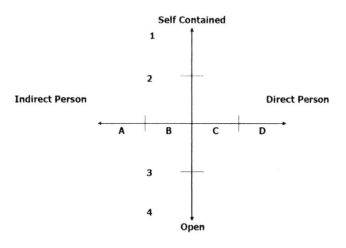

Figure 6.3 Defining your Selling & Buying Styles

If you scored 1 or 2 and C or D – then you fit into the **Driver** category.

If you scored 3 or 4 and C or D – then you fit into the **Expressive** Category.

If you scored 1 or 2 and A or B – you fit into the **Analytical** category.

If you scored 3 or 4 and C or D – you fit into the **Amiable** category.

The Driver:

The Driver shows outward signs of purpose. They are very determined to succeed and have a "Can Do" attitude. They have tremendous inner certainty and everything is based around "do it now." The Driver is a risk taker and makes decisions very quickly. Drivers love the feeling of power and control, and are impatient with people who do not keep up with their pace. They are not the greatest of listeners and tend to have moved on to the next item if the current one is not stimulating them any more.

The Expressive:

The Expressives are fun lovers. They are very enthusiastic about the possibilities for the future. Expressives tend to have tremendous vision and are creative. In Stephen Covey's book, "The Seven Habits of Highly Effective People," one of the habits is: "Begin with the end in mind". This habit is clearly seen by the Expressives because of their creativity. A disadvantage of an Expressive is that they do not like detail. They become bored with routine and want to move onto something a lot more exciting.

The Analytical:

One of the first areas to be aware of when dealing with the Analytical is have your facts right. In my early days of selling I can remember being told that you never send out information to a prospect, you just arrange the appointment. With the Analyticals you really need to send information because that is the basis on which they make decisions. Analyticals can appear to be slow to build relationships. However when they do you really have a customer for life. They ask a lot of detailed questions because they deem that to be very important.

The Amiable:

When you are working with or selling to the Amiables it is very important to relate to their values. The Amiable is the team player and will always be interested in possibilities. They are, however, slow to change and they do not like surprises. The Amiables are always very receptive to an approach, but will not always tell you what they are really feeling. They value good customer service and will always stay in touch with people. The Amiable is very receptive to the consultative sales approach.

When you consider your existing customers you should take note of the personality style they display over the years, I have learnt to adapt and modify my style to assist me in building greater rapport with other personality styles. In order to complete greater levels of business, you need to increase your rapport levels – to do this it is important to analyse what motivates the different personality styles.

Now that you have made your appointment with a new prospect, let us have a look at how you recognise different styles when you first meet the prospect. We get clues from their office environment, the words they use and the body language signals they display.

Recognising Buying Styles

	Driver	Expressive
Office Environment	• Large Leather Chair • Certificates of Individual Achievements • Executive Toys	• Colourful Office • Pictures taken with famous people • Desk may be a mess • Plenty of books about building relationships • Networking certificates
Words They Use	• "What's the bottom line?" • "How long will this take?" • "I'll tell you what we need to do"	• "Great to see you" • "I have an open door policy" • "We have to look at the bigger picture"
Body Language	• Walking round office • Very strong eye contact • Strong hand movements	• Open hand gestures • Plenty of smiles • Watch for glazed eyes if conversation becomes too detailed

Recognising Buying Styles

	Amiable	Analytical
Office Environment	• Warm feel to office • Plenty of plants • Pictures of family • Pictures of team achievement • Might be an open plan office	• Tidy and clinical look to office • Certificates of technical achievement • Plenty of technical manuals in the office
Words They Use	• "Thanks for coming in to see us" • "What is your opinion on........ • "We need to keep this in line with our company values"	• "Do we have an agenda for this meeting" • "How can we find a practical approach to this problem" • "That is appropriate"
Body Language	• Watch for nods of agreement • Relaxed persona • Excellent listening skills	• Lack of eye contact • Taking notes • Observe long periods of silence

Figure 6.4 – Recognising Buying Styles

With this information you will be able to recognise an individual's personality style and subsequently be able to modify your approach to suit the differing styles. Here is how you can modify that approach.

Approaching the Buying Styles

Approaching Buying Styles Through The Sales Cycle		
	Driver	**Expressive**
Approaching	• Be direct and assured. Get straight to the point	• Be open and friendly. Talk about them.
Questioning	• Ask questions around achievement and bottom line.	• Use questions that paint pictures.
Presenting	• Be factual and assertive	• Use stories of other peoples experience using your product
Completing	• State alternatives and use action words.	• Allow them to express how your product will be of to benefit them
Dealing With Indifference	• Meet resistance with reflective questions	• Encourage them to re-visit the concept of your product

Approaching Buying Styles Through The Sales Cycle		
	Amiable	**Analytical**
Approaching	• Slow the pace and be very responsive to feelings.	• Be well prepared and have your technical details organised.
Questioning	• Ask their opinion and feelings to general areas.	• Ask structured questions and take notes.
Presenting	• Get regular feedback and relate to personal values.	• Give plenty of details and time for prospect to review.
Completing	• Relate to the team and how it will help them.	• Give alternatives and time to analyse.
Dealing With Indifference	• Be careful and be responsive to their feelings.	• Give alternatives with detail.

Figure 6.5 – Approaching the Buying Styles

Having the techniques to assist you in building greater rapport with your existing and potential customers you are in a position to find out how you can help them achieve their goals using your product or service.

Here is further reading on Personality Styles and Buying & Selling Styles:

"Personal Styles & Effective Performance" by David Merrill and Roger Reid

"The Writings, Works and Books" of Dr Anthony Alessandra.

Main Takeaways From Chapter 6:

- There are emotional & logical reasons to buying
- Always have a structure to & agenda for your sales meetings – this increases the likelihood of success
- Recognising the different buying styles & their traits is a skill well worth developing as it makes it easier for you to build the all important rapport & trust.

Chapter 7

– Relationship Selling Skills

Topics Covered:

- The Opening Statement
- Questioning Technique
- Platforming
- The Gap Analysis
- Confirm Your Understanding
- Presenting To Win
- Features, Advantages & Outcomes
- The Four Types Of Business Completion
- Late Resistance & How To Deal With It

The Opening Statement

Quite simply, there has to be a clear and communicated message of what the expectations are for a Sales meeting. If a prospect has a misguided belief that you will try to sell them something that they do not feel they need or want, do not be surprised if there is resistance. It is imperative that you clearly and succinctly communicate your objectives for the meeting. Is the meeting just to speak generally about what you do or is it to complete a full fact find of their needs and wants? Or is business to be completed at the meeting?

Anyone who uses the line: "I am not here to sell you anything," should be very careful because that is exactly what you want to do. We are all in the world of selling. A better approach would be: "I would love to do business with you, however if I am to do so, it is important to me to do it properly."

An opening statement should clearly outline the following:

1. How this meeting will go
2. The objective at the end of the meeting
3. The next stage (where you go from there)

A suggested opening statement might be as follows:

"Many thanks for meeting with me today. The purpose is to establish how, we as a company, may be able to assist you to achieve your goals and objectives. I would like to ask you a number of questions and, at the end of the meeting, I will, with your permission, prepare a proposal that we can discuss at a future meeting."

As you are still at the early stages of your first meeting your prospect is still sizing you up. They will be very quick to recognise competence or incompetence. Another opening statement could be:

"The purpose of this meeting is for you to tell me what you deem to be of importance in your business, so that I can have a better insight into helping you to fulfil your goals and aspirations."

Questioning Technique

The ability to get on your prospect's map of the world is the key to helping them achieve their goals. Under the new method of selling, once you have built rapport you have permission to ask questions that in turn, will give you the permission to make a presentation.

Eliciting Values

Ask yourself this question: "Why do you do what you do?" A powerful question when you consider it. During my business-coaching meetings that question is regularly asked and you would be amazed at the differing answers received. In fact some people have never given the question any thought at all.

When you elicit people's values you have utilised the greatest rapport building technique of all. We all have values and when we help people fulfil those values we are in a state of excellent rapport. In order to elicit values, here are some powerful questions to use.

"In the context of your business, what's important to you?"

"When it comes to your relationship with our company, what's important to you?"

"When it comes to the future, what is important to you?"

"When it comes to money, what is important to you?"

When you have elicited the framework of values you are in a position to help your prospects set goals that your product or service will help them achieve. The key to helping your prospect identify those goals is having the ability to ask probing questions.
Before we get to the art of questioning, think back to the days when you were about three years of age. At that age you started asking probably the most probing question of all time – the question WHY?

Children have a huge craving for information so they have no inhibitions about the questions they ask. Not only that, they will also ask the why question to whomever they like, sometimes to the complete embarrassment of their parents. "Why has that man got black teeth Daddy?" This one questions when asked, and if accepted, gives a child more information. However, as you know, most children at that age are not content with the answer to the first question. They will make it their business to probe even further.

If we think about it the "why?" question is how children start to learn about all sorts of subjects. Unfortunately, we are discouraged from maintaining this form of questioning as we get older because it means we are being too inquisitive for our own good. The reality in selling is that to be inquisitive we must be very confident because by being inquisitive we receive information from your prospects that you can use to prepare a proper presentation,

As the great Rudyard Kipling said: "I keep six honest men serving. They taught me all I knew. Their names are What, Why, When, How, Where and Who." Effective selling means thinking with a child's inquisitiveness and always asking the "why?" question. Over and over.

Platforming

Platforming is used to ensure that you see the aspirations and goals fears and doubts exactly the same way as your prospect. If you were to ask your prospect a specific open question, for example: "What are your feelings towards providing a quality service to your clients?" Obviously their reply will be that they deem it to be very important. If at that stage we feel we understand exactly what our prospects means by "very important" we start to make assumptions and ultimately will make a presentation based upon those assumptions. With the technique of platforming we never assume that we have enough information and we always want to probe, and be even more inquisitive, just like we were when we were children. In order to understand what the prospect means by "very important" we can ask a further question. "When you say very important, how do you mean?"

Early in my sales career I learnt to ask that question: "How do you mean". That one question has given me more specific information than I ever thought was possible. Now for all you English language scholars you will have noticed that this question is grammatically incorrect. It should, in fact, be: "What do you mean?" The challenge with, "What do you mean," is that it can sound somewhat impertinent, whereas, "How do you mean," is much softer and, provided we have developed the levels of trust and rapport required, we will, without doubt, elicit the information to enable us to make a specific presentation.

The "How do you mean" question allows you have a complete understanding of your prospect's needs and wants and this is imperative. When you go into a meeting you know only the details of how your product or services work. You know nothing about your prospect, their goals and aspirations for the future and, ultimately, how your product or service will be of real benefit in meeting their specific requirements.

Asking open questions continually is very powerful. If you notice chat show hosts and interviewers, they are exceptional in eliciting information from their guests and they also possess that brilliant ability to think on their feet. Open questions are used to gather information. You can never ask enough of them, but this should be done only when you have rapport and trust. If you do not have sufficient levels of rapport and trust, it does not matter what question you ask.

The key to the relationship method of selling is when asking these questions that you check where your prospects are in terms of making a decision or series of decisions. This means that through the use of closed questions you will be able to confirm their current position. When you do this there is no misunderstanding of their needs and aspirations. In the Old Method of Selling the key was to build up to a big closing situation. The "move forward – check position" method allows you maintain the high level of rapport and trust required, mainly because you will not be surprising them with a wonderfully prepared closing technique.

In confirming your current position, questions like:

"Would that be important to you?" or, "Is that something that might be of interest to you?" are good questions to use and ascertain where your prospects are at in their decision making process. Remember you are there to do business but on a long term basis, so we always need to be sure that we are proceeding properly.

The GAP Analysis

The P.RO.S.P.E.R.© Consultative Selling Method

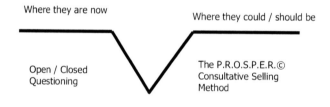

Where they are now

Where they could / should be

Open / Closed Questioning

The P.R.O.S.P.E.R.© Consultative Selling Method

Figure 7.1 The P.R.O.S.P.E.R© Consultative Selling Method

Are your customers achieving all they want by using your product or service? Are your current prospects achieving all that they want by using your competitor's product or service? Nobody is ever 100 per cent happy with the product or service they are using. The GAP Analysis is specifically designed to identify where your prospect or customer is currently and across the divide where they want to be. Remember the three types of prospect/customer that you come across.

1. The prospect/customer who knows they have a need and they want to do something about it. In this situation the GAP is identified and they are very often the type of people who will call you, if they are aware of your product, to buy from you.

2. For the prospect who knows they have a need, however they do not want to take action, the GAP is actually identified – however there is reluctance to bridge that GAP.

3. For your prospects that do not even realise that they have a need, there is no GAP identified, by which your skill of questioning may identify an opportunity to bridge that GAP

The P.R.O.S.P.E.R© Consultative Selling Method

Here is a very effective questioning technique you can utilise to assist you identify the GAP. When wanting to understand a prospects needs and wants, the P.R.O.S.P.E.R© Consultative Selling Method is a great way to stay in control of your fact find meeting.

P	Positioning
R	Realities
O	Objectives
S	Shortfalls
P	Pathways
E	Effects
R	Rewards

Positioning

Positioning is a great way to deliver your Opening Statement and setting the agenda for the meeting. A way to do this might be to say to your prospect "Let me tell you what I propose we do at this meeting". You might also include the following - "I would love to find out what you do and how you do it and from that we might be able to find ways for you to do it better." When you position the meeting, your prospect has a clear understanding of the agenda for the meeting.

Realities

At this stage you ask your prospect all the questions that pertain to what they are doing at present, or indeed what products they are currently using in their business. A good question at this stage would be "Tell me about what the current situation is here at the ABC Company?" Or another: Tell me about what products you are currently using?"

You might at this stage find out from them what they feel or think of their current supplier by asking them questions like "Tell me what would you like to improve in what you are currently using?" By asking this question you are identifying the GAP between where they are and where they would ultimately like to be.

As discussed earlier, the big challenge we all face in selling is the status quo and the prohibitor to change is indeed the "fear of change." By identifying what changes are needed, we are starting to identify the reasons why a prospect might consider doing business with us, now or at some stage in the future.

Objectives

This is the part in the GAP Analysis where you can identify the ultimate objective in dealing with a current supplier; or in the future have dealings with you and your company. A great question you can ask at this stage is "In an ideal situation what do you look for in a supplier to your company?" While we have discussed that no prospect is ever 100% happy with any supplier, this is a great opportunity to identify the differences in what they want and what they are getting currently.

Another question you can ask at this stage which will identify the GAP: "If you had a free hand to make any improvements to what you have, what would they be?" This is a great question for a prospect who is particularly unhappy with their current supplier. All of the above is of course dependant on where you are when it comes to building and maintaining rapport and trust.

Shortfalls

In this part of the consultative selling method you are now identifying the difference or differences in where they are currently and where they could or should be by using your product or service. You may need to re-cap those differences with your prospect or it may already have been made clear by them during your questions. If you have to re-cap at this stage, let them know what you have identified before moving to pathways.

Pathways

At this stage you start to look at options or pathways that will enable your prospects to consider how you could assist them in achieving their goals and objectives. Your prospects will also be looking for signals from you to demonstrate how you can deliver on your promises if they are to consider making a change in supplier. You can also promote the fact that if they give you a try, you can have some degree of risk reversal. This can eliminate any "fear of change" that your prospect has.

Effects

By making this change or improvement to you as a supplier or vendor your prospect is now starting to look at the improvement this will make to their business. A question you might consider asking at this stage would be "In an ideal situation, if we could help you make these improvements, how will this effect the development of your business?" People are always looking to do things more effectively and or efficiently and this question identifies what the effects or efficiencies are.

Rewards

The buyer will make a decision for two reasons – the effect the decision will have on the organisation and how they will be perceived for making that decision. You may actually elicit this personal reward to the buyer or it may remain silent. Rewards can be just the personal recognition within the organisation by helping it make the right decision.

Overall the P.R.O.S.P.E.R© Consultative Selling Method is a great structure to allow you understand your prospects needs, goals and objectives and will enable you to understand before being understood. Write the 7 letters of PROSPER down the left hand side of a sheet of paper and bring the sheet with you to your meeting and structure your questions accordingly.

Listening Skills

For some people this seems to be a real challenge. While it is understandable that we want to let our prospects know all about our products and services, they have little interest in the technicalities and details of the product, unless it fills a particular need and want for them- remember WII-FM. (What's in it for me?) When you listen very closely, and platform extensively, the real reason why your prospect wants to do business specifically with you is revealed.

In Dr Stephen Covey's best selling book, "The Seven Habits of Highly Effective People", one of the habits is: "Seek first to understand, then to be understood." By listening closely we can understand and be understood through our presentation.

To help you listen more closely, here is a method you can use. For those of you that find listening over extended periods a challenge, this method will take continuous practice, but just watch the results that follow.

When somebody is giving you information, repeat the words over in your mind consciously exactly as they say them. Doing so minimises the chance of you wandering in your own mind. Have you ever been in a situation talking with someone when suddenly they get that "glazed look in their eye"? They may be losing interest, or they may just be internalising for themselves something that you said which sent them off on a tangent.

To bring them back to listening mode is, ask another question to confirm your prospect's understanding. At this stage in the sales process it is very necessary for us to be continually asking questions.

Confirm Your Understanding

Summarising your understanding of what is important to a prospect having listened to them in their business is a wonderful way of creating and maintaining empathy with them. Remember your prospects and clients do not care what you know until they know that you care.

Once you have built good rapport and trust with your prospect, you in effect have permission from them to ask questions. Always ask your prospect can you take notes. No matter how good your memory is, you will seldom remember everything that you have heard.

Presenting To Win

Now that we have dealt with 70 per cent of the process involved in the New Method of Selling, we are in a position to make a proper and formal presentation. We can encourage our prospect to complete business with us.

Before we get into this crucial part of the sales cycle there are two things to bear in mind:

1. People do not buy your product or service. They buy what your product will do for them.

2. People act to gain a reward or to avoid a penalty.

When you have created rapport and asked sufficient questions in order to be in a position to make this presentation, it is important you use a process called Features, Advantages and Outcomes

Features, Advantages and Outcomes

To understand fully the reasons why people purchase from you, as opposed to your competitors, it is important for you to grasp the following technique. The ability to successfully feedback the information identified at questioning time shows a huge degree of empathy in the selling process. It also shows that you have utilised your active listening skills. Let us consider a scenario.

Imagine that you are returning home and are driving an old BMW. The car is starting to get a bit tired. You are late for a meeting and go to overtake an articulated lorry. Once you get to the point of no return another truck comes over the brow of the hill towards you. Putting a foot to the accelerator you just about get back to your own side of the road "in the nick of time". What thoughts would go through your head? Whilst somewhat animated, they would be likely to be along the lines of "it is time to change my car."

A few days later you pass a BMW Main Dealer and in the showroom window is a brand new BMW 330CI. Going into the showroom to enquire about it you are greeted by Sales Person No 1.

He greets you and proceeds to detail all the wonderful features of this fantastic car.

"This car has a double overhead camshaft, fuel injection system, side impact bars, double airbags, anti skid control and climate control etc..."

He then lets you know that should you require any further information about the car, he will be in his office. He heads off while you continue to view the car, somewhat confused by all the features just outlined.

With that a second Sales Person No.2 approaches   not knowing that Sales Person No.1 had already been talking to you. He greets you in a welcoming manner.

He then proceeds to ask the following:

Sales Person: "What are your first impressions of the car?"

You: "It is a fine car, style-wise."

Sales Person: "Would you mind if I asked a few questions?" (Confirming my interest level).

You: "No please feel free."

Sales Person: "When it comes to motoring, what is important to you?"

You: "Well the first thing is safety and the second is performance when needed."

Sales Person: "Tell me what are you driving currently?"

You: "I have an 8-year-old BMW."

Sales Person: "Are you thinking of changing your car at the moment?"

You: "I am thinking of it."

Sales Person: "Tell me why you are thinking of changing?"

You: "I was returning for a meeting and was running late. I went to overtake an

	articulated lorry and another one came over the brow of the hill and I just managed to get back to my side of the road in the nick of time."
Sales Person:	"On the information you have just given me, I can tell you that the main feature of this BMW 330Ci is the fuel injection system. The fuel injection system allows the engine to be supplied on demand with the petrol necessary for performance. The advantage of this is that it solves the problem of you being able to get back to your side of the road in the nick of time. The real outcome for you is that you have the safety and performance that is important to you."

Which Sales Person will I buy the BMW 330CI from? Sales Person No.1 explained all the wonderful features of the car but neglected to ask what you were looking for in a car. Sales Person No.2 was consultative in his approach as his goal was only to present the main feature of the car to me.

When presenting the Features, Advantages and Outcomes of your particular product or service, here is a guide to assist you.

Feature:	This explains what your product, or service, does. It is general information. It is not specific to an individual's needs and/or wants.
Advantages:	Solves a problem, or creates an opportunity. When you are eliciting information with your questioning technique, you will find the problem to be solved, or the opportunity to be created.

Outcomes:	By solving the problem, or creating the opportunity, your prospect will gain a reward or avoid the penalty.

Please refer to the exercises in the Appendices of this book and apply this technique to your industry, product or service.

As discussed at the beginning of the book, the Old Method of Selling was branded as an aggressive type of selling, where closing was everything. The new method of selling has much more to do with facilitating the needs and wants of prospects and customers with your product or service.

The challenge with the new method of selling is that some people become passive in their approach to asking for the business and find instead that it goes to a competitor. When all is said and done, it is very important that we ask for the business and also that we deal with any reservations a prospect or client may have.

The Four types of Business Completion

1. The "Ask for It" Close

   This is very straight-forward where you just ask the following question: "Are you happy to proceed with the business?" Another question you could ask is: "Where are you at in your decision making process?"

2. The Assumptive Close

   This is where we automatically assume that the business is being proceeded with. Phraseology you could use with this method might be: "Let's get the paperwork organised," or, "Let's get the car delivered for you." This is a very direct method of closing the business and very effective, for instance, with the buying style of The Driver.

3. The Alternative Close

When you give people alternatives they will, having identified a need or want and provided trust and rapport are present, decide on one of them. For example: "Would you like to begin this plan from today, or will we backdate it to the beginning of the month?" or, "Do you want to pay by cheque, or would direct debit suit you better?" Another closing sentence might be: "Would you like delivery of the car in red, or do think black is more desirable?"

4. The "Minor Detail" Close

At this stage when your prospect is deciding the benefits of engaging your product or service, you can assist the process by helping them focus on a minor detail. For example: "Are you happy with the layout of the kitchen area?" (minor detail when purchasing a complete house). Once they have agreed with you, then revert to the "Ask for it" Close or the Assumptive Close.

It is important to stress that there are only a few ways of asking for the business. Over the years having had experience of many closing techniques on training programmes, I found most of them were impractical and probably never used in the real marketplace.

It is important however to make the point that it is better to have many closing techniques, as opposed to being afraid to ask for the business at all. Let's face it, your prospect and customer is actually waiting to be asked. Do not disappoint them.

Late Resistance & How To Deal With It

Finally, it is critical to be able to deal with buying resistance while, at the same time, keeping the ongoing customer relationship uppermost in our minds.

There are four main reasons why your prospect sometimes shows resistance at this stage in the process.

1. Some people do not like making a decision. They are afraid of making the wrong one and sometimes you need to help them to feel comfortable to make their decision.

2. Some people have a reasonable doubt. It is legitimate for your prospect to have some resistance, and we have to be able to respond to and deal with these doubts. Remember we want to continue doing business with our customers.

3. Some people didn't understand. Your prospects are not going to tell you that they did not understand your proposition. They will just tell you that they want to consider or think about your offer.

4. Some people have hidden reasons. You may never know what some people are thinking and you always wonder why some people were procrastinating about doing business with you. It could be that you were not in rapport with them and did not want to say it.

Here is a five stage approach for dealing with resistance.

1. Listen to the Objection

It is imperative at this stage that you listen very closely to the concerns that your prospect has. You have arrived at this stage in the process and you want the business.

2. Cushion the objection and acknowledge its worth

Use the "Feel, Felt Found" technique to cushion their concerns.

"I appreciate how you feel at present and some of my best clients felt the same way at this stage also, however when we were able to deal with their concerns, we found they were happy to proceed in doing business."

3. Condition prospect's mind to receive a logical answer

When dealing with buyer resistance try to establish that the objection they have given you is the real one and that you haven't been given a side objection. Do this by asking them: "If I can clear up your concerns, will you be happy to proceed with the business?" If at this stage you find there are still concerns it is useful to establish from your prospect where they are in their decision making process.

4. Present the Answer

On the basis that you have the real barriers to your prospect completing the business, revert back to the Features, Advantages and Outcomes technique.

5. Complete The Business

When you have dealt with their concerns the completion of the business should be straightforward.

In conclusion, there is a very fine line between being assertive with your prospect and them having the feeling that you are being unduly aggressive in your approach. If people want to think genuinely about your proposition, you must allow them to do so, however be sure you have an agreed process for follow up. It is my firm belief that closing and completion is a formality and the real sale has already taken place when you not only developed rapport and trust with a prospect but maintained it

Main Takeaways From Chapter 7:

- Be very clear in communicating your message – not just for a sales meeting, but at all times
- Eliciting your prospects or clients values will make doing business considerably easier
- The "Why?" question is crucial in establishing detailed knowledge of your prospects needs & wants
- Platforming – walking in your clients shoes
- Utilise the P.R.O.S.P.E.R© Consultative Selling Method
- Develop strong listening skills – they will enable you to more easily (& appropriately) complete business
- Always confirm your understanding of a clients needs or wants with them
- Using the Features, Advantages & Outcomes approach will help you close many deals
- Learn to deal respectfully with late resistance – you will either overcome it there and then or withdraw without damaging your existing rapport & trust – allowing you to return in the future.

Epilogue

I hope you have enjoyed "The Book On Relationship Selling". I believe that coaching for salespeople in the future will be enabling them to build relationships built on real rapport and trust with customers, relationships that will be "win win" for both parties. But to achieve this **rapport** is the key.

Today, we see career sales people who earn large incomes and who do not depend on the organisation they work for or with, to be successful. These people work very independently with their clients coaching them to achieve their challenging goals.

To all relationship salespeople I say be very proud of the profession you are in. You always keep the wheels of business turning.

If you would like more information on how to achieve your goals or find out how Sales Coaching can assist you, please feel free to contact me at: jonathan@achieve-prosper.com

I look forward to hearing from and working with you. In the meantime, truly I wish you the very best of luck in relationship selling.

Yours in Prosperity!

Jonathan Bell

Appendix 1 (1 of 3)

Exercises Re Principles of Relationship Selling (Chapter 1)

Exercise 1

Please list below the names of ten new suspects for your business

	Suspect Name
1.	
2.	
3.	
4.	
5.	
6.	
7.	
8.	
9.	
10.	

Exercise 2

What three actions do you need to take to qualify these suspects as prospects?

	Actions
1.	
2.	
3.	

Exercise 3

List below ten existing customers or clients you can sell more of your product or service to over the next six weeks.

	Customer
1.	
2.	
3.	
4.	
5.	
6.	
7.	
8.	
9.	
10.	

Appendix 1 – Continued (3 of 3)

Exercise 4

Please list below additional products you will introduce to these existing customers.

	Additional Product
1.	
2.	
3.	
4.	
5.	

Exercise 5

Please now outline three ways that you can sell more frequently to your existing customers.

	More Frequent Selling
1.	
2.	
3.	

Exercises Re The Inner Game of Selling & The Power of Goal Setting
(Chapters 2 & 3)

Exercise 1

What are your three greatest strengths in the field of selling?

	Greatest Selling Strengths
1.	
2.	
3.	

What are your three greatest challenges in the field of selling?

	Greatest Selling Challenges
1.	
2.	
3.	

Exercise 2

List three victories in your sales career that raised your self esteem.

	Self Esteem Raising Victories
1.	
2.	
3.	

List three areas that are fun about your sales career.

	Fun Areas Of My Sales Career
1.	
2.	
3.	

Exercise 3

What are the five most important things to you about your selling career?

	Important Things Of My Sales Career
1.	
2.	
3.	
4.	
5.	

Exercise 4

List five goals you will to achieve in the next year

	Goals
1.	
2.	
3.	
4.	
5.	

When you achieve the above goals what does that mean to you personally?

	Meaning Of Goals
1.	
2.	
3.	
4.	
5.	

Exercise 5

Having clarity of vision for your selling career is a wonderful quality. Athletes use visualisation techniques every day of their careers. Please now take a trip in time five years from now and outline what is happening in your sales career. Write everything in the present tense as if is happening right now. (Guidelines to help you start writing would be for example: Where are you living? What are you driving? What is your annual income?) Let your pen run free.

Exercise 6

Please now list some of our achievements you have accomplished in your life and career. Concentrate on achievements that heightened your feelings at the time – remember only your impression of the event counts.

Achievement	Impressions
1.	
2.	
3.	
4.	
5.	

Exercises Re Prospecting And Making Appointments (Chapters 4 & 5)

Exercise 1

List below the three differences your product/services make from your competitors.

	Product / Service Differentiation
1.	
2.	
3.	

List below three qualities that differentiate you personally from your competitors.

	Personal Quality Differentiation
1.	
2.	
3.	

Exercise 2

List below five customers whom you feel would be the easiest to ask for referrals.

	Easiest Customers To Ask For Referrals
1.	
2.	
3.	
4.	
5.	

List below five customers whom you feel would be the most challenging to ask for referrals.

	Most Challenging Customers To Ask For Referrals
1.	
2.	
3.	
4.	
5.	

Exercise 3

Develop a referral script to support the previous question.

Referral Script

Exercise 4

Prepare your phraseology with a view to making an appointment with a new prospect via telephone.

Introduction

Interest

Iither/Or

Exercise 5

When preparing your approach to a new prospect there is a certain formality required. Prepare your approach to an existing customer and you decide how formal it needs to be.

Introduction

Interest

Either/Or

Appendix 3 – Continued (5 of 6)

Exercise 6

Please consider alternative adjectives to the following:

	Alternative
Feel	
Felt	
Proud	

Exercise 7

Outline your phraseology using the "Feel, Felt and Found" technique to deal with the objection "I'm not interested" from a prospect.

Exercise 8

Outline your phraseology for the 99% approach.

```
_____
_____
_____
_____
_____
_____
_____
_____
_____
_____
_____
```

Exercises Re Building And Maintaining Rapport With Customers
(Chapter 6)

Needs and Wants/The Rapport Building Process

Exercise 1

List ten customers with whom you feel you have the greatest rapport

	Customer
1.	
2.	
3.	
4.	
5.	
6.	
7.	
8.	
9.	
10.	

What percentage of your overall annual business is achieved from the above customers?

_____%

Exercise 2

List your ten customers with whom you have the least amount of rapport.

	Customer
1.	
2.	
3.	
4.	
5.	
6.	
7.	
8.	
9.	
10.	

What percentage of your overall business is achieved from this category of customers?

_____%

Appendix 4 – Continued (3 of 4)

Exercise 3

The opening of the sale is structured into four areas. What percentage of your time is spent on these areas?

	%
Building Rapport	
Opening Statement	
Questioning	
Listening	

Exercise 4

Identify the five prospects with whom you have the least amount of rapport.

	Prospect
1.	
2.	
3.	
4.	
5.	

Appendix 4 – Continued (4 of 4)

Exercise 5

Please outline five ideas for assisting you to build rapport with the prospects that you listed in Exercise 4.

	Idea
1.	
2.	
3.	
4.	
5.	

Exercises Re Relationship Selling Skills
(Chapter 7)

Exercise 1

Design five open questions to assist you with gathering more information about your customers needs and wants.

	Open Question
1.	
2.	
3.	
4.	
5.	

Exercise 2

Closed questions are also referred to as trial closes. Outline five closed questions that you will use to confirm information and commitment.

	Closed Question
1.	
2.	
3.	
4.	
5.	

Exercise 3

List your top five customers and using the GAP analysis identify where they are now with regard to a product/service and where they could be by purchasing a new product /service.

Customer	Now	Could Be

Exercise 4

Utilise the P.R.O.S.P.E.R© Consultative Selling Method to identify G.A.P.

P

R

O

S

P

E

R

Exercise 5

Listening exercise.

For an evening, work at listening carefully to a friend or member of your family. Then list your five main observations.

	Listening Observation
1.	
2.	
3.	
4.	
5.	

Exercise 6

Identify an item you purchased recently and, more importantly, why you purchased that item.

Reason for purchase (Why)

Identify what reward you gained by your purchase.

Identify what penalty you avoided by your purchase.

Exercise 7

Identify three reasons why a customer is "better off" by purchasing your product/service.

	Why Better Off?

Exercise 8

When you assist your customers to save time or money there is a strong possibility of them doing more business with you. Identify in what way your prospects suffer loss of time or money by not using your product/service.

	Why Your Prospects "Suffer"

Exercise 9

Identify four of your products and identify the main feature of each of them. State the advantages and benefits of each of them.

Product	Main Feature	Advantages	Benefits

Exercise 10

When asking for the business it is very important that you are clear and deliberate with your phraseology. Please prepare responses using the four main closes.

The "Ask for it" Close

The "Assumptive" Close_

The "Alternative" Close

The "Minor Detail" Close

Exercise 11

As we have seen not everyone is prepared to close straight away for various reasons. Please now list five of the type of objections you are likely to be offered.

	Objection
1.	
2.	
3.	
4.	
5.	

Exercise 12

Dealing with prospect's objections while keeping the potential client relationship uppermost in our minds is a well balanced skill. With the response to objections used in this module, please outline how you will deal with the indifference to close the sale.

Objection	Response

Bibliography & Recommended Reading

"The Writings, Works And Books" Dr. Anthony Alessandra

"Multiple Streams of Income" – Robert G Allen

"Promptings" – Kody Bateman

"How To Win Friends And Influence People" – Dale Carnegie

The Seven Habits of Highly Effective People – Dr Stephen R Covey

"Selling to Win" – Richard Denny.

"How to Master the Art of Selling" – Tom Hopkins

"The Cashflow Quadrant" – Robert Kiyosaki

"Appreciation Marketing" – Tommy Wyatt & Curlis Lewsy

"Psycho Cybernetics" – Dr Maxwell Maltz

"Swim With The Sharks, Without Being Eaten Alive" – Harvey McKay

"Personal Styles & Effective Performance" – David Merrill & Roger Reid

"Selling to The Top" – David Peoples

"The Success System That Never Fails" – W. Clement Stone

"I Will" – Ben Sweetland

"Referral Of a Lifetime" – Tim Templeton

"Maximum Achievement" – Brian Tracy

"Advanced Selling Strategies" – Brian Tracy

"The New Dynamics of Winning" – Dr Denis Waitley

"Psychology of Winning" – Dr Denis Waitley

"The New Dynamics of Goal Setting" – Dr Denis Waitley

Jonathan's Recommended Resources

Send Out Cards – A Referral Marketing & Stay in Touch Greeting Card system – www.sendoutcards.com/59230

Oprius – An excellent Contact Management System for Independent Sales Professionals

www.achieve-prosper.com/opriusCRM.htm

Success Studios Corporation – Online Goal Setting Software

www.achieve-prosper.com/goalpro.htm

BNI (Business Network International) – The Global Referral Organisation – www.bni.com

Thomas International – Identify your Selling Style
www.thomasinternational.net

Rich Dad, Poor Dad – Plan your route to financial freedom
www.richdad.com

Nightingale Conant – A fantastic resource for Selling CD's and mp3 downloads.

www.achieve-prosper.com/nightingaleconant.htm

Jonathan's Seminars, Conference Keynotes & One-to-One Coaching Programmes

Conference Keynotes – (40 mins – 2 Hours)

Win/Win More Business
Enter the Performance Zone – The "Inner Game of Selling"
Growing your Business by Referral – A 5 Step Plan

Seminars & Workshops (Half Day – 2 Days)

The "Stay Motivated for Selling" Seminar.
Prospecting for Results
Perfecting the Face-to-Face Meeting – The P.R.O.S.P.E.R©
Consultative Selling Method.
Understanding Buying & Selling Styles.
The Propser Referral Marketing System Workshop
Presentation Skills for Profit
Serve & Prosper – Customer Care Programme

One-to-One Coaching & Mentoring. (Project & Contract Basis)

Sales Director Leadership Programme
Sales Management Coaching for Sales Managers
Sales Coaching for Prosperity Programme

For more details please contact:

jonathan@achieve-prosper.com

Infodex Page